"Drawing on her landmark, two-decade-long study of the adult children of divorced parents, Ahrons, one of this country's foremost authorities on marriage and family therapy, rebuts the argument that divorce inevitably damages children psychologically and emotionally, and offers sound, sensible advice about how divorcing couples can promote their children's well-being after a marriage dissolves. Invaluable reading for anyone who has been divorced or who has experienced their parents' divorce."

> —Steven Mintz, John and Rebecca Moores Professor of History,
> University of Houston, and author of *Domestic Revolutions: A Social History of American Family Life*

"Absolutely essential for everyone concerned with divorce and its effects on children. Grounded in scientific research and years of clinical experience, this is a compassionate and refreshing antidote to doomsayers who exaggerate the perils of divorce, presented by a leading authority on divorce. Filled with insights and advice that will pay huge dividends to divorced parents and their children. An astounding accomplishment. If you want the best for your children, read this book."

> —Richard A. Warshak, Ph.D., clinical professor of Psychology,
> University of Texas Southwestern Medical Center,
> and author of *Divorce Poison: Protecting the Parent-Child Bond from a Vindictive Ex*

"With clarity, compassion, insight, and humor, Dr. Ahrons gives us a blueprint to follow so that children can thrive and even flourish as they emerge from divorce, become adults, and start their own families. *We're Still Family* beautifully presents solid research that answers questions that have plagued families and clinicians alike!"

> —Lois Braverman, president,
> American Family Therapy Academy,
> and author of *Women, Feminism, and Family Therapy*

"A welcome surprise for contemporary families who will learn that divorce does not have to destroy families nor damage children. Without the usual stereotypes or clinical biases, Ahrons documents the complexities of divorced families from the responses of the children of divorce, now grown up with families of their own, and tells us what works and what does not."

> —Pauline Boss, professor, University of Minnesota
> and author of *Ambiguous Loss*

We're Still Family

We're Still Family

What Grown Children Have to Say About Their Parents' Divorce

Constance Ahrons, Ph.D.

HarperCollins*Publishers*

HarperCollins books may be purchased for educational, business, or sales promotional use. For information, please write: Special Markets Department, HarperCollins Publishers Inc., 10 East 53rd Street, New York, NY 10022.

FIRST EDITION

Designed by Jaime Putorti

Printed on acid-free paper

Library of Congress Cataloging-in-Publication Data
Ahrons, Constance R.
    We're still family : what grown children have to say about their parents' divorce/Constance Ahrons.—1st ed.
        p. cm.
    Interviews with adult children from the divorced families originally studied in the author's *The Good Divorce,* © 1994.
    Includes bibliographical references and index.
    ISBN 0-06-019305-0
        1. Divorce—United States—Longitudinal studies. 2. Adult children of divorced parents—United States—Interviews. I. Title.
HQ834.A675 2004
306.89—dc22
                                                                                          2003067609

04 05 06 07 08 ❖/RRD 10 9 8 7 6 5 4 3 2 1

To the families who have honored me by sharing their lives
and
To my mentor, anthropologist Paul Bohannan,
who led the way

CONTENTS

INTRODUCTION

In the past year alone, every major newspaper has featured articles bemoaning the high divorce rates, blaming divorce for the demise of the American family and for dooming children to lifelong problems. With divorce rates hovering around 50 percent for over thirty years now, two generations of children have experienced divorce as common. Yet despite a lack of any reliable evidence, the old, stereotyped images of children of divorce as emotionally troubled, drug abusing, academically challenged, and otherwise failing to thrive persist.

Let's close the newspaper, turn off the TV and think about it for a moment. When we read that divorce *causes* children to have serious problems, it's as if "divorce" is a singular event made up of some "average" experience. Between my clinical work, my research, my students, my friends and my family, I've known thousands of divorces and I've never met an average one. The average divorce, or the average family, for that matter, is an artifact of our need to oversimplify complex issues.

When we read the headlines that tell us that "on average" or "all things being equal" kids fare better in two-parent families than in other family forms, we have to ask ourselves, what does this really mean for my child, my family or myself? Does it mean that, given two families with *the same* resources—emotional, financial, social and community—and children with *the same* innate, environmental and social resources, children who don't experience divorce have the edge over those who do? It doesn't take long to see how meaningless such statements are, because the infinite subtle variations in individual differences preclude our ability to hold *all things equal.*

The media will always tend to shine a spotlight on worst-case scenarios. After all, bad news sells while good news is boring. The truth is that families are too complex and too individual to justify these kinds of overgeneralized conclusions.

Imagine for a minute that your family is like an egg. When you break the protective shell the ingredients emerge. Now you've got some choices. You can poach it, fry it, or scramble it. But whatever way you cook it, you've still got an egg. It's the same with families. Families are far more than their fragile shells. The protective shell—the household—may be broken, but the major ingredients—the children, their needs and your relation- ship with them—are still the same. Ending a marriage is a painful, wrenching process that shakes up the family's foundation, but it doesn't follow that the family itself is broken. How you rearrange the ingredients, how two new households are built from the original foundation, is the key to the family's future.

This book tells the story about what really happens to families and in particular to children when parents decide to divorce. I draw on in-depth interviews with 173 adult children who experi- enced the divorce of their parents over twenty years ago. You will hear how their lives changed and what lasting effects divorce had on them. I have been working with, studying, and teaching about divorced families for the past three decades, and I can tell you that, contrary to the headlines, divorce doesn't destroy families. Instead, it has the unique potential to rearrange them, preserving meaningful parent-child relationships and expanding to include new relatives gained through parents' remarriages. While no one goes into a marriage hoping it will end in divorce, families *can* and *do* adapt and thrive in the face of change.

Take Jessica, a thirty-year-old lawyer, married mother of two, who was eight when her parents divorced nearly twenty-two years ago. By the time her fourteenth birthday rolled around, Jessica had accumulated two stepsisters, one stepbrother, a half-brother, a halfsister, a stepmother, a stepfather, two stepgrandmothers, one stepgrandfather, and a menagerie of stepaunts, -uncles and -cousins. Although Jessica's family doesn't fit the familiar tidy image we call family, it does all the things other families do and it is much more common than most of us realize. Over one-quarter of adults between the ages of twenty-one and forty experienced a parental divorce during their growing-up years and now have families that resemble Jessica's. Her family represents a new kind of normal.

But if you are contemplating or in the midst of a divorce, it's natural to want to know what it's going to be like for your kids to grow up in a complex family. What are the benefits? The losses? What do the relationships really look like? Do children of divorce feel they have half as many family members or twice as many? Is there a legacy that children of divorce carry into adulthood? Do they still view themselves many years later through a prism of divorce?

Why do some adult children of divorce fare so much better than others? What is it about the parents, the children or the divorce process itself that contributes to these differences? And why, in some families, is one child resilient while another becomes a victim?

These are the questions we will explore in the following pages.

HOW THIS BOOK CAME TO BE

In 1994 I wrote a book called *The Good Divorce*, which was based on a study I had done of parents and stepparents who were interviewed three times during the first five years after divorce. In that book I highlighted the huge variations in how families reorganize after divorce. I found good divorces and bad ones and dozens of variations in between. I found amicable exspouses who had worked out cooperative parenting relationships and angry exspouses who, even after five years, could not effectively share parenting of their children. The findings and the perspective I took in that book showed that divorce did not need to destroy families and that, in fact, many parents formed parenting partnerships after divorce that permitted them to meet the needs of their children. My research was met with opposition from those arguing that divorce destroyed families and had dire negative effects on *all* children. They claimed that children of divorce failed to achieve in school, in relationships and life in general. By the early 2000s, the national debate about divorce was heating up once again. After three decades of important hard-won divorce reforms, such as the introduction of no-fault divorce laws and joint custody legislation, a new backlash reform movement was gaining momentum. Proposals are now emerging to rescind no-fault legislation, calling it a "social experiment" that failed. Claims that joint custody is bad for children are growing, *based on little or no evidence.*

This is not to suggest that there haven't been good studies. In fact, research on divorce has increased substantially over the past few decades, but translating good solid knowledge from esoteric academic journals to the general public is difficult. The available research about the impact of divorce and separation on children has generated useful knowledge, but it also has led to confusion and misunderstanding. Because divorce is such a hot, value-laden issue, complex realities become submerged in polarized discussions.

However, divorce is neither good nor bad. These extreme positions bury the accumulating body of findings that reveal a more nuanced picture of divorce, one that defies sound-bite conclusions.

Garnering most of the media attention, however, has been a twenty-five-year study conducted by Judith Wallerstein. Painting a very grim picture, Wallerstein claims that children of divorce are doomed to have serious problems that persist, worsening over the years and casting a dark shadow on their adult lives. What is most disturbing is her claim that her subjects are representative of typical American middle-class families.

Although the description of her original sample of sixty Marin County, California, families is suspiciously absent from her recent book, it appears in the appendix of her first book. Recruited through newspaper ads and flyers, divorced parents were offered counseling services in exchange for their participation in the research. Many that volunteered and became participants in her study had serious psychological problems. As noted in the appendix of *Surviving the Breakup*, "fifty percent of the men and close to half of the women . . . were chronically depressed, sometimes suicidal individuals, the men and women with severe handicaps in relating to another person, or those with long-standing problems in controlling their rage or sexual impulses." She and her coauthor, Joan Berlin Kelly, go on to say that an additional "15 percent of the men and 20 percent of the women were found by us to be severely troubled during their marriages, perhaps throughout their lives." They "had histories of mental illness including paranoid thinking, bizarre behavior, manic depressive illnesses, and generally fragile or unsuccessful attempts to cope with the demands of life, marriage, and the family."

That a small sample of sixty such troubled families has made headlines and given rise to sweeping conclusions about the long-term effects of divorce only attests to our fascination with bad news. While Wallerstein presents an elegant portrayal of children's pain, with poignant stories and intense, heartrending reactions, her conclusions about the harm divorce causes are exaggerated and not as widespread as she claims them to be. Clearly, a study in which two-thirds of the parents range from the chronically depressed to the seriously mentally ill is not a representative sample. Reporting on the worst-case scenarios ensures that you'll hear the worst stories. Given how seriously impaired many of their parents were, it is highly unlikely that the divorce itself accounts for all of the adult children's struggles she describes.

Although Wallerstein's findings are discredited in academic circles, they are still greeted with enthusiasm by the divorce reform movement. It feeds them with just the ammunition they need to pursue their fight to restore the traditional family by saving marriages and making divorce more punitive. This small, select sample is still being used to prove that "the unexpected legacy" of divorce is the insidiously harmful ways it leaves its mark decades afterward.

One has to wonder, what about the children whose divorced parents are mentally healthier than those Wallerstein studied? Do children in these divorced families experience their growing-up years differently from those in troubled families? As adults how do they evaluate their lives?

It was this omission that made me decide to continue my study. I had written numerous academic articles and two books about divorce but in recent years I had set my research aside. Now that the issue of the long-term effects of divorce on children was being vigorously debated, I knew I needed to resume my study, this time with the adult children. Although studies about the effects of parental divorce on young children and adolescents are numerous, long-term perspectives have been scarce because there simply hasn't been an adequate adult population to study. But now that divorce has been with us for several decades, we at last have the opportunity to hear from children who have grown up with divorce as a fact of their lives and have gone on to make families and relationships of their own. Their voices reveal truths about divorce's effects on kids.

Back in 1979, when I first began the study, I was on the faculty at the University of Wisconsin. With a grant from the National Institute of Mental Health I used a typical research approach to ensure that the sample was representative of the population of divorced parents in one Midwestern county over a six-month period. My goal was to interview one hundred families, and based on statistics that can tell how large a population is needed to assure a certain number of subjects, I randomly selected every fourth name. The importance of this random selection from a general pool of divorces is that the study better represents the population because the sample mimics the variety of divorces we are likely to see in that population.

The divorced couples I first interviewed in 1979 had over two hundred children, now ranging in age from twenty-one to forty-seven, and finding them two decades later proved a challenge. They were scattered across the country by now and of course many had families of their own. Much to my surprise, however, fully 90 percent consented to be interviewed. These grown-up children of divorce knew about my original interviews with their parents and stepparents and wanted to be heard about how they felt about their parents' divorces, how it impacted their lives and how they felt about living in the new families created by divorce.

What I heard from them is that not only did they survive their parents' divorces but the vast majority thrived, despite the stress and upheaval that are common in the early stages of parental divorce. The majority told us that they felt that their families were normal and their relationships with each of their parents had actually improved. As adults—most in intimate relationships themselves, some married, others cohabiting, still others looking for mates—most felt their parents' divorce was a good decision and that both they and their parents were better off because of it. Others spoke of warm relationships with their stepparents and shared happy stories of joyful celebrations that included both their biological and stepparents. Of course a small minority did not fare as well. They felt the divorce had deprived them of family, and as adults they felt their lives were worse off accordingly.

If you experienced your parents' divorce as a child, I expect that you will find comfort in knowing how others like you reacted to their parents' divorce. But, more important, you will learn that it is never too late to accept your parents' divorce and make the most of the family you have, even if it's not the perfect family you had hoped for. *How you view* your parents' divorce, their marriage, and their remarriages also has important implications for you as you create intimate relationships in your own life. It matters in terms of who you marry, how good your marriage is, how you resolve conflict, how you feel about divorce in your own life, and how you parent.

What was perfectly clear from speaking at length with these adults is that many decisions parents make when they rearrange the family can either make it better or worse for the children— such things as how you tell your kids about the separation, what kind of living and custody arrangements you make for them, how flexible or rigid these arrangements are, how often the kids see their fathers, how they feel about their parents' dating and new partners, how remarriages are handled, what it feels like to have an "instant" new family. One of the most consistent comments was that *how parents relate to each other,* both during the marriage and long after, makes the biggest difference of all.

As I sifted through the transcripts of the interviews, I realized that these adult children could provide an invaluable blueprint for what works in these rearranged families and what doesn't. That's why I wrote this book.

WHAT YOU CAN EXPECT
IN THE PAGES TO COME

In Part I, I show how specific myths about divorce negatively impact divorced parents and their children and why it's important to dispel them. The questions asked of the adult children in my study about who they are today, how they feel about their lives, their intimate relationships, whether they wish their parents were still together and how they feel now about their parents' divorces reveal interesting and surprising answers.

In Part II, I explore the complex changes children experience after divorce and what worked and didn't work for the children we spoke with. Their living arrangements and how and why they changed over the years offer important insights for parents. As they share their views of their parents' dating, remarriages and re-divorces we learn how stepparents and new siblings impact their lives. They trace surprising changes in their parents' relationships over twenty years and give poignant examples of how their family tribes participated in their weddings and holiday celebrations. Many of these adults now have children of their own, and how the divorce impacts this next generation attests to the importance of having a long-range view of divorce. How their parents related— and still continue to relate, whether they are hostile or amicable, emerges as a major theme, subtly affecting almost all aspects of their lives.

The final section of this book is devoted to the understanding of resilience, why and how some children thrive while others do not. I spell out how parents and adult children can increase resilience, showing that it is never too late to have a good divorce and invest in parenting. In closing, the adult children have the final say and offer the wisdom of their hindsight. I then take on the fact that families cannot do this in isolation and suggest what societal changes are needed to build stronger families rearranged by divorce.

If you are a divorced parent, or one contemplating divorce, you know how difficult it can be to imagine how the way you rearrange your life now will forever change not only your life but your children's as well, and that can be an awesome responsibility. Each day you will face decisions that simply weren't relevant during the marriage. Where will the children live and how often will they see each parent? Will both of you, and perhaps stepparents, attend the soccer playoffs? A few years later, the questions and choices will change again: It may be, How do I tell my children I am getting married and that they will soon have a stepparent and two stepsisters? A few more years pass, and your fourteen-year-old daughter wants to go live with her father and his new family, and you don't want her to. What to do? Listening to the adult children of divorce as they chronicle the changes and talk about their feelings will help you make the difficult and confusing decisions that are a normal part of living with divorce.

You will also have the unique opportunity to hear from those who grew up in joint and sole custody arrangements, as well as from siblings. The perspectives of the different siblings show so clearly not only that divorce affects children differently but that *even children in the same family react differently.* Of course if you are a parent of more than one child, you already know that your kids react differently to the same experiences. Sometimes it's related to age, birth order or gender, but more often it's simply a matter of temperament and the different relationships they had with you and your spouse *prior to* the divorce. By taking into consideration the fact that your kids will respond differently to the divorce and to the arrangements you make, you can better understand and make decisions tailored to their individual needs.

It's normal to feel as if you're flailing around, trying to devise a plan that will suit everyone's needs. In fact it may not be possible; what children want, and even need, often conflicts with what you and your former spouse want and need. But the twenty-twenty hindsight of these young adults provides important guidelines that can help you reconfigure your family in the best possible way, thereby helping your children thrive by reducing both the immediate stresses and the possibilities of long-term negative effects.

It is important to remember that children also have internal and external resources *outside* of the family that have the power to mediate the impact of the divorce. Different temperaments and different qualities such as intelligence, social skills and physical characteristics help determine how individual children respond to change and stress. Friends, family, teachers, coaches and neighbors all can be important resources in helping them cope. It is also simply a fact that some children are more resilient to life's stresses than others.

As you read this book you will find that there is no perfect family, with or without a divorce. But you will also see that some families meet children's needs better than others, and as you understand how and why, you can apply what you have learned to your own situation. You'll also see that even if you make mistakes early on, it is never too late to help your children on their journey to adulthood. Even though it's not possible to do all the right things all the time, in all likelihood your children will still be fine and often will understand and respect the work you did to try to improve their lives. Even many years later, when the divorce seems like distant history, it is still possible to make changes that will help your family relationships be more satisfying for yourself, your ex, and your children.

Part One
The Truth About Divorce

Chapter 1

NO EASY ANSWERS

Why the Popular View of Divorce Is Wrong

"Everyday meat and potato truth is beyond
our ability to capture in a few words."

ANNE LAMOTT, *BIRD BY BIRD*

It was a sunny, unseasonably warm Sunday morning in October. In a quaint country inn in New Jersey, surrounded by a glorious autumn garden, my young grandchildren and I waited patiently for their Aunt Jennifer's wedding to begin. The white carpet was unrolled, the guests were assembled, and the harpist was playing Pachelbel's Canon.

A hush came over the guests. The first member of the bridal party appeared. Poised at the entry, she took a deep breath as she began her slow-paced walk down the white wedding path. Pauline, my grandchildren's stepgreat-grandmother, made her way down the aisle, pausing occasionally to greet family and friends. A round of applause spontaneously erupted. She had traveled fifteen hundred miles to be at her granddaughter's wedding, when only days before, a threatening illness made her presence doubtful.

Next in the grand parade came the best man, one of the groom's three brothers. Proudly, he made his way down the aisle and took his position, ready to be at his brother's side. Then the two maids of honor, looking lovely in their flowing black chiffon gowns, made their appearance. My grandchildren started to wiggle and whisper: "It's Aunt Amy [my younger daughter]! And Christine [the longtime girlfriend who cohabits with Uncle Craig, my daughters' halfbrother]!" As they walked down the aisle and moved slowly past us, special smiles were exchanged with my grandchildren—their nieces and nephew.

Seconds later, my youngest granddaughter pointed excitedly, exclaiming, "Here comes Mommy!" They waved excitedly as the next member of the bridal party, the matron of honor—*their mother, my daughter*—made her way down the path. She paused briefly at our row to exchange a fleeting greeting with her children.

Next, the groom, soon officially to be their "Uncle Andrew," with his mother's arm linked on his left, and his father on his right. The happy threesome joined the processional. Divorced from each other when Andrew was a child, his parents beamed in anticipation of the marriage of their eldest son.

Silence. All heads now turned to catch their first glimpse of the bride. Greeted with oohs and aahs, Aunt Jennifer was radiant as she walked arm in arm with her proud and elegant mother, their stepgrandmother, Grandma Susan. Sadly missed at that moment was the father of the bride, my former husband, who had passed away a few years earlier.

When I told friends in California I was flying to the East Coast for a family wedding, I stumbled over how to explain my relationship to the bride. To some I explained: "She's my exhusband's daughter by his second wife." To others, perhaps to be provocative and draw attention to the lack of kinship terms, I said, "She's my daughters' sister." Of course, technically she's my daughters' halfsister, but many years ago my daughters told me firmly that that term "halfsister" was utterly ridiculous. Jennifer wasn't a half anything, she was their *real* sister. Some of my friends thought it strange that I would be invited; others thought it even stranger that I would travel cross-country to attend.

The wedding reception brought an awkward moment or two, when some of the groom's guests asked a common question, "How was I related to the bride?" With some guilt at violating my daughters' dictum, but not knowing how else to identify our kinship, I answered, "She is my daughters' halfsister." A puzzled look. It was not that they didn't understand the relationship, but it seemed strange to them that I was a wedding guest. As we talked, a few guests noted how nice it was that I was there, and then with great elaboration told me stories about their own complex families. Some told me sad stories of families torn apart by divorce and remarriage, and others related happy stories of how their complex families of divorce had come together at family celebrations.

At several points during this celebratory day, I happened to be standing next to the bride's mother when someone from the groom's side asked us how we were related. She or I pleasantly answered, "We used to be married to the same man." This response turned out to be a showstopper. The question asker was at a loss to respond. First and second wives aren't supposed to be amicable or even respectful toward one another. And certainly, first wives are not supposed to be included in their exhusband's new families. And last of all, first and second wives shouldn't be willing to comfortably share the information of having a husband in common.

Although it may appear strange, my exhusband's untimely death brought his second and first families closer together. I had mourned at his funeral and spent time with his family and friends for several days afterward. A different level of kinship formed, as we—his first and second families—shared our loss and sadness. Since then, we have chosen to join together at several family celebrations, which has added a deeper dimension to our feelings of family.

You may be thinking, "This is all so rational. There's no way my family could pull this off." Or perhaps, like the many people who have shared their stories with me over the years, you are nodding your head knowingly, remembering similar occasions in your own family. The truth is we are like many extended families rearranged by divorce. My ties to my exhusband's family are not close but we care about one another. We seldom have contact outside of family occasions, but we know we're family. We hear stories of each other's comings and goings, transmitted to us through our mutual ties to my daughters, and now, through grandchildren. But if many families, like my own, continue to have relationships years after divorce, why don't we hear more about them?

Quite simply, it's because this is not the way it's supposed to be. My family, and the many others like mine, don't fit the ideal images we have about families. They appear strange because they're not tidy. There are "extra" people and relationships that don't exist in nuclear families and are awkward to describe because we don't have familiar and socially defined kinship terms to do so. Although families rearranged and expanded by divorce are rapidly growing and increasingly common, our resistance to accepting them as normal makes them appear deviant.

Societal change is painfully slow, which results in the situation wherein the current realities of family life come into conflict with our valued images. Sociologists call this difference "cultural lag," the difference between what is real and what we hold as ideal. This lag occurs because of our powerful resistance to acknowledging changes that challenge our basic beliefs about what's good and what's bad in our society.

WHY GOOD DIVORCES ARE INVISIBLE

Good divorces are those in which the divorce does not destroy meaningful family relationships. Parents maintain a sufficiently cooperative and supportive relationship that allows them to focus on the needs of their children. In good divorces children continue to have ties to both their mothers and their fathers, and each of their extended families, including those acquired when either parent remarries.

Good divorces have been well-kept secrets because to acknowledge them in mainstream life threatens our nostalgic images of family. If the secret got out that indeed many families that don't fit our "mom and pop" household ideal are healthy, we would have to question the basic societal premise that marriage and family are synonymous. And that reality upsets a lot of people, who then respond with familiar outcries that divorce is eroding our basic values and destroying society.

Although we view ourselves as a society in which nuclear families and lifelong monogamous marriages predominate, the reality is that 43 percent of first marriages will end in divorce. Over half of new marriages are actually remarriages for at least one of the partners. Not only have either the bride or groom (or both) been divorced but increasingly one of them also has parents who are divorced.

Families are the way we organize to raise children. Although we hold the ideal image that marriage is a precursor to establishing a family, modern parents are increasingly challenging this traditional ideal. Families today arrange—and rearrange—themselves in many responsible ways that meet the needs of children for nurturance, guidance and economic support. Family historian Stephanie Coontz, in her book *The Way We Never Were*, shows how the "tremendous variety of workable childrearing patterns in history suggests that, with little effort, we should be able to forge new institutions and values."

One way we resist these needed societal changes is by denying that divorce is no longer deviant. We demean divorced families by clinging to the belief that families can't exist outside of marriage. It follows then that stories of healthy families that don't fit the tidy nuclear family package are rare and stories that show how divorce destroys families and harms children are common. In this way, bad divorces appear to represent the American way of divorce and good divorces become invisible.

MESSAGES THAT HINDER GOOD DIVORCES

When the evils of divorce are all that families hear about, it makes coping with the normal transitions and changes that inevitably accompany divorce all the more difficult. Negative messages make children feel different and lesser, leading to feelings of shame and guilt. Parents who feel marginalized in this way are less likely to think about creative solutions to their problems. That all of this unnecessary anxiety is fueled by sensationalized reports of weak findings, half-truths and myths of devastation is deplorable. Only by sorting out the truths about divorce from the fiction can we be empowered to make better decisions, find healthy ways to maintain family relationships, and develop important family rituals after divorce. Let's take a close look at the most common misconceptions about divorce.

Misconception 1:
Parents should stay married for the sake of the kids

This is a message that pervades our culture, and it rests on a false duality: Marriage is good for kids, divorce is bad. Underlying this premise is the belief that parents who divorce are immature and selfish because they put their personal needs ahead of the needs of their children, that because divorce is too easy to get, spouses give up on their marriages too easily and that if you're thinking about divorcing your spouse, you should "stick it out till the kids are grown." A popular joke takes this message to its extreme. A couple in their nineties, married for seventy years, appears before a judge in their petition for a divorce. The judge looks at them quizzically and asks, "Why now, why after all these years?" The couple responds: "We waited until the children were dead."

The research findings are now very clear that reality is nowhere near as simple and tidy. Unresolved, open interparental conflict between married spouses that pervades day-to-day family life has been shown again and again to have negative effects on children. Most experts agree that when this is the case it is better for the children if parents divorce rather than stay married. Ironically, prior to the initiation of no-fault legislation over twenty years ago, in most states this kind of open conflict in the home was considered "cruel and inhumane" treatment and it was one of the few grounds on which a divorce would be granted—if it could be proved.

But the majority of unsatisfying marriages are not such clear-cut cases. When most parents ask themselves if they should stay married for the sake of their children, they have clearly reached the point where they are miserable in their marriages but wouldn't necessarily categorize them as "high-conflict." And here is where, in spite of the societal message, there is no agreement in the research findings or among clinical experts. That's because it's extremely complex and each individual situation is too different to allow for a "one-size-fits-all" answer.

A huge list of factors comes into play when assessing whether staying married would be better for your kids. For example,

- Is the unhappiness in your marriage making you so depressed or angry that your children's needs go unmet because you can't parent effectively?

- Do you and your spouse have a cold and distant relationship that makes the atmosphere at home unhealthy for your children?
- Do you and your spouse lack mutual respect, caring or interests, setting a poor model for your children?
- Would the financial hardships be so dire that your children will experience a severely reduced standard of living?

Add to this your child's temperament, resources and degree of resilience, and then the personal and family changes that take place in the years after the divorce, and you can see how the complexities mount.

It is a rare parent who divorces *too easily*. Most parents are responsible adults who spend years struggling with the extremely difficult and complex decision of whether to divorce or stay married "for the sake of the children." The bottom line is that divorce is an adult decision, usually made by one spouse, entered into in the face of many unknowns. Without a crystal ball, no one knows whether their decision will be better for their children. As you read further in this book, however, you may gain some perspective on what will be most helpful in your situation, with your children, by listening carefully to the reactions and feelings of various children of divorce *as they have changed over twenty years.*

Misconception 2: "Adult children of divorce" are doomed to have lifelong problems

If your parents divorced when you were a child, you are often categorized as an ACOD, an "adult child of divorce," and we all know there's nothing good to be said about that. I dislike this label because it is stigmatizing. It casts dark shadows over divorcing parents and their children, results in feelings of shame and guilt, and is another way of pathologizing divorce.

Years ago I coined a term, "divorcism," to call attention to the stereotypes and stigma attached to divorce. To put children with divorced parents in a special category is divorcism in action. It stereotypes them as a group with problems, and like all stereotypes it ignores individual differences.

If your parents didn't divorce, are you then called an "adult child of marriage"? No, you're just "normal." Normal kids must have two parents of different genders who live in the same household; anything else is abnormal, and if you're abnormal then you must be dysfunctional. That's the way the American family story goes.

Perhaps the worst outcome of this labeling is that it makes parents and children feel that this one event has doomed them and they don't have the power to change anything. This pinpointing of divorce as the source of personal problems is pervasive. Parents worry that whatever problems their kids have, even when they are normal developmental issues, were caused by the divorce. Children are encouraged to blame the divorce for whatever unhappiness they may feel, which makes them feel helpless about improving their lives. Teachers are often too quick to identify divorce as the reason for a child's school behavior problem. The greater society points a finger at divorce as the reason for a wide range of greater social problems.

The truth is that, for the great majority of children who experience a parental divorce, the divorce becomes part of their history but it is not a defining factor. Like the rest of us, most of them reach adulthood to lead reasonably happy, successful lives. Although children who grew up with divorced parents certainly share an important common experience, their ability to form healthy relationships, be good parents, build careers, and so on, are far more determined by their individual temperaments, their sibling relationships, the dynamics within their parents' *marriages* and the climate of their *postdivorce* family lives.

Misconception 3:
Divorce means you are no longer a family

There's this myth that as long as you stay married your family is good but as soon as you announce you're separating, your family is thrown into the bad zone. Your family goes from being "intact" to being "dissolved," from two-parent to single parent, from functional to dysfunctional. Even though we all know that people don't jump from happy marriages right into divorce, there is an assumption that the decision to separate is the critical marker. It doesn't seem to matter whether your marital relationship was terrible, whether you were miserable and your children troubled. Just as long as you are married and living together in one household, the sign over the front door clearly states to the world, "We're a normal family."

The inaccurate and misleading message that divorce destroys families is harmful to both parents and children because it hides and denies all the positive ways that families can be rearranged after divorce. It sends the destructive message to children that divorce means they only get to keep one parent and they will no longer be part of a family. Although two-parent first-married households now represent less than 25 percent of all households, and an increasing number of children each year are raised by unmarried adults, many people cling to the belief that healthy families can only be two-parent married families and social change is always bad and threatening to our very foundations.

When Julie, one of the participants in my study, married recently, she walked down the aisle with a father on either side. On her left was her biological father, on her right was her stepfather of eighteen years. Her mother was her matron of honor, who joined her former and present husbands, all standing together to witness the marriage. Two best men, the groom's eleven-year-old twin sons from his first marriage, stood next to him. Helen, the groom's former wife, sat close by, accompanied by Tony, her live-in partner.

While this wedding ceremony doesn't fit the traditional pattern, Don and Julie have joined the three-quarters of American households who have living arrangements other than that of the "traditional" family.

My older daughter thanked me for coming to Jennifer's wedding. She told me that my being there made it possible for her to share this happy occasion with *all* her family, instead of feeling the disconnections that some children feel in divorced families. This bonding spreads to the third generation so that my grandchildren know us all as family.

The truth is that although some divorces result in family breakdown, the vast majority do not. While divorce changes the form of the family from one household to two, from a nuclear family to a binuclear one, it does not need to change the way children think and feel about the significant relationships within their families. This does not mean that divorce is not painful or difficult, but over the years, as postdivorce families change and even expand, most remain capable of meeting children's needs for family.

Misconception 4:
Divorce leaves children without fathers

This message is linked closely with the preceding one because when we say that divorce destroys families we really mean that fathers disappear from the family. The myths that accompany this message are that fathers are "deadbeat dads" who abandon their kids and leave their families impoverished. The message strongly implies that fathers don't care and are unwilling or unable to make continuing commitments to their children. While this reflects the reality for a minority of divorced fathers, the majority of fathers continue to have loving relationships with their children and contribute financially to their upbringing.

The truth is that many fathers do spend less time with their children after divorce, but to stereotype them as parents who abandon their children only creates more difficulty for both fathers and their children. It establishes a myth that men are irresponsible parents who don't care about their children, when in reality most feel great pain that they are not able to see their children more frequently. In the vast majority of divorces, over 85 percent, mothers are awarded sole custody, or in the case of joint custody, primary residence. This means that most fathers become nonresidential parents after divorce. Being a nonresidential father is a difficult role with no preparation or guidelines.

Most of the research on dads after divorce focuses on absentee fathers, while involved fathers are frequently overlooked. Many fathers continue to be excellent parents after divorce and in fact some fathers and children report that their relationships actually improve after the divorce. In much the same way that good divorces are invisible in the public debate, so are involved fathers.

Misconception 5:
Exspouses are incapable of getting along

When I first started to study divorce in the early 1970s, it was assumed in the literature that any continuing relationship between exspouses was a sign of serious pathology, an inability to adjust to the divorce, to let go and to move on with their lives.

In the late 1970s, when joint custody was first introduced, it was met with loud cries of skepticism from the opposition. How could two parents who couldn't get along well enough to stay married possibly get along well enough to continue to share parenting? Two decades ago I confronted the skeptics by writing several articles arguing that we needed to accept the reality of our divorce rates and needed to transform our values about parenting after divorce. The issue was no longer *whether* divorced parents should share parenting to meet their children's needs but *how*.

Although there have been many legal changes over the years, and some form of joint custody legislation exists now in all states, questions about its viability still prevail. These accusations, citing joint custody as a failed "social experiment," are not based on research findings, which are still very limited and inconclusive, but instead on the ill-founded stereotype that all divorcing spouses are bitter enemies, too lost in waging their own wars to consider their children. Certainly this is true for some divorcing spouses, the ones that make headlines in bitter custody disputes, but it is not true for the majority.

Although we have come to realize that parents who divorce still need to have some relationship with one another, the belief that it's not really possible still lingers. In fact, when exspouses remain friends they are viewed as a little strange and their relationship is suspect. Yet, the truth is that many divorced parents *are* cooperative and effective coparents. Like good divorces and involved fathers, they are mostly invisible in the media.

Despite much resistance, joint custody has become increasingly common, and new words, such as "coparents," have emerged in response to this reality. The newest edition of *Webster's College Dictionary* (2000) recognizes the term, defining it as separated or divorced parents who share custody and child rearing equally. While I don't agree that coparenting is limited only to those parents who share child rearing equally, or even that those who coparent need to share equally in time or responsibility, the inclusion of the word in the dictionary sanctions important new kinship language for divorced families, thereby advancing our ability to acknowledge complex family arrangements.

Misconception 6: Divorce turns everyone into exfamily; in-laws become outlaws

When it comes to the semantics of divorce-speak, all of the kinship ties that got established by marriage dissolve abruptly. On the day of the legal divorce, my husband and all of his relatives suddenly became exes. But even though the kinship is *legally* terminated, meaningful relationships often continue. My friend Jan, during her fifteen-year marriage, formed a very close relationship with her mother-in-law. Now, twenty years later, she still calls her eighty-two-year-old exmother-in-law "Mom," talks with her several times a week and has dinner with her weekly. Exmother-in-law is certainly not an adequate description of this ongoing relationship.

As a culture we continue to resist accepting divorce as a normal endpoint to marriage even though it is an option chosen by almost half of those who marry. It is this cultural lag, this denial of current realities that causes the inaccurate language, not only for the family ties that continue but also for the family we inherit when we, our former spouses, our parents or our children remarry. Kinship language is important because it provides a shorthand way for us to identify relationships without wading through tedious explanations.

We have terms like "cousin," "great-aunt" or uncle, and "sister-in-law" that help us quickly identify lineage in families. Even these kinship terms are sometimes inadequate and confusing. For example, "sister-in-law" can mean my brother's wife, or my husband's sister, or my husband's brother's wife. And even though you don't know exactly *how* she is related to me, you do at least know that she belongs in the family picture. The in-law suffix quickly tells you that we are not blood relatives but we are related through marriage lines.

Our failure to provide kinship language that recognizes some kind of viable relationship between parents who are no longer married to each other, as well as language that incorporates old and new family as kin, makes children feel that their identity is shattered by divorce. It is no wonder that we remain in the dark ages when it comes to normalizing complex families after divorce and remarriage.

Our language and models for divorce and remarriage are inadequate at best, and pejorative at worst. Relegating the relationship between divorced spouses who are parents to the term "exspouse" hurls children and their parents into the dark territory of "exfamily." The common terms of "broken home," "dissolved family," and "single-parent family" all imply that children are left with either no family or only one parent.

This lack of positive language is one more way that the invisibility of good divorces impacts postdivorce families.

Misconception 7: Stepparents aren't real parents

One of the implications of the high divorce rate is that the shape and composition of families have changed dramatically in the last twenty years. All over the world, weddings no longer fit the traditional model: there are stepparents, half siblings, stepsiblings, stepchildren, intimate partners of parents, stepgrandparents and even, on rare occasions, exspouses of the bride or groom.

To complicate the wedding picture even more, one or both of the bride and groom's parents may have been divorced. And given that well over half of those who divorce eventually remarry, we are likely to find that the majority of those who have divorced parents also have stepparents. Add the dramatic increase in cohabitation to that equation and it is not unusual for an "unmarried intimate partner" of one of the parents to be present as well. These complex families require photographers to quickly switch to their wide-angle lens and totally revamp their traditional formats for wedding photos.

Over half the children today have adults in their lives for whom they can't attach socially accepted kinship terms. They lack social rules that would help them know how they are supposed to relate and how to present these adults to the social world around them. I am reminded here of a *Herman* cartoon, showing a boy holding his report card and asking his teacher: "Which parent do you want to sign it: my natural father, my stepfather, my mother's third husband, my real mother or my natural father's fourth wife who lives with us?"

As the cartoon clearly suggests, there are real and natural parents, and then there are stepparents. Stepmothers are stereotyped in children's literature as mean, nasty and even abusive. The only time we hear about stepfathers is when the media highlights the sensationalized case of sexual abuse. Added to these negative images is the reality that stepparents have no legal rights to their stepchildren. The research on stepparents is still very limited and positive role models are lacking.

Children and their new stepparents start off their relationships with two strikes against them. They have to fight an uphill battle to overcome negative expectations, and they have to do so without much help from society. Since almost 85 percent of the children with divorced parents will have a stepparent at some time in their lives, it is shocking that we know so little about how these relationships work. Clearly, societal resistance to recognizing the broad spectrum of postdivorce families has hindered the development of good role models for stepchildren and their stepparents.

Painting a False Picture

Taken together, these negative messages paint a false picture of divorce, one that assumes family ties are irretrievably broken so that postdivorce family relationships appear to be nonexistent. Despite these destructive messages, many divorced parents meet the needs of their children by creating strong families after divorce. Without a doubt, divorce is painful and creates stress for families, but it is important to remember that most recover, maintaining some of their kinship relationships and adding new ones over time.

By making good divorces invisible we have accepted bad divorces as the norm. In so doing, children and their divorced parents are being given inaccurate messages that conflict with the realities they live and make them feel deviant and stigmatized. It is time we challenge these outdated, ill-founded messages and replace them with new ones that acknowledge and accurately reflect current realities.

THE DISTORTIONS OF OVERSIMPLIFYING

Just a little over a decade ago, in January 1989, the *New York Times* Magazine ran a cover story called "Children after Divorce," which created a wave of panic in divorced parents and their children. Judith Wallerstein and her coauthor, Sandra Blakeslee, a staff writer for the *New York Times,* noted their newest unexpected finding. Calling it the "sleeper effect," they concluded that only ten years after divorce did it become apparent that girls experience "serious effects of divorce at the time they are entering young adulthood."

When one of the most prestigious newspapers in the world highlights the findings of a study, most readers take it seriously. "That 66 percent of young women in our study between the ages of nineteen and twenty-three will suffer debilitating effects of their parents' divorce years later" immediately became generalized to the millions of female children with divorced parents. The message—just when you think everything may be okay, the doom of divorce will rear its ugly head—is based on a *mere eighteen out of the grand total of twenty-seven women* interviewed in this age group. This detail wasn't mentioned in the fine print of the article but is buried in the appendix of the book that was scheduled for publication a month after the *New York Times* story appeared. And it is on this slim data that the seeds of a myth are planted. We are still living with the fallout.

In sharp contrast to Wallerstein's view that parental divorce has a powerful devastating impact on children well into adulthood, another psychologist made headlines with a completely opposite thesis. In her book, *The Nurture Assumption: Why Children Turn Out the Way They Do,* Judith Rich Harris proposes that what parents do makes little difference in how their children's lives turn out. Half of the variation in children's behavior and personality is due to genes, claims Harris, and the other half to environmental factors, mainly their peer relationships. For this reason, Harris asserts parental divorce is not responsible for all the ills it is blamed for.

These extreme positions — of divorce as disaster and divorce as inconsequential — oversimplify the realities of our complex lives. Genes and contemporary relationships notwithstanding, we have strong evidence that parents still make a significant difference in their children's development. Genetic inheritance and peer relationships are part of the story but certainly not the whole story.

SORTING OUT THE RESEARCH FINDINGS

Drawing conclusions across the large body of research on divorce is difficult. Studies with different paradigms ask different questions that lead to different answers. A classic wisdom story shows the problem. Three blind men bumped into an elephant as they walked through the woods. They didn't know what it was, but each prided himself on his skill at "seeing." So one blind man reached out and carefully explored the elephant's leg. He described in great detail the rough, scratchy surface that was huge and round. "Aha, this is an ancient mighty tree. We're in a new forest." "No, no," said the blind man who had taken hold of the elephant's trunk. "We're in great danger—this is a writhing snake, bigger than any in our hometown. Run!" The third man laughed at them both. He'd been touching the elephant's tusk, noticing the smooth hard surface, the gentle curve, the rounded end. "Nonsense! We have discovered an exquisitely carved horn for announcing the emperor's arrival."

The blind men described what they "saw" accurately. Their mistake was to claim that what they saw was the whole. Much like the three blind men, researchers see different parts of the divorce elephant, which then frames their investigations.

It should come, then, as no surprise that reports of the findings about divorce are often contradictory and confusing. It is impossible for any study to take account of all the complexities of real life, or of the individual differences that allow one family to thrive in a situation that would create enormous stress, and frayed relationships, in another. But it is in these variations that we can begin to make sense of how divorce impacts the lives of individuals and families.

FACING REALITY

Hallmark Cards recently launched a line of greeting cards called "Ties That Bind" aimed at various nontraditional unions—from stepfamilies to adopted child households to unmarried partnerships. "Our cards reflect the times," says Marita Wesely-Clough, trend group manager at Hallmark. "Relationships today are so nebulous that they are hard to pin down, but in creating products, we have to be aware that they are there. Companies need to respect and be sensitive to how people are truly living their lives now, and not how they might wish or hope for them to live."

Advertising agencies and marketing services make it their business to assess social realities. To sell their products, they have to evaluate the needs and desires of their potential consumers. They do not share the popular cultural anxiety about the changes in families. Instead they study them and alter their products to suit. Policy makers would do well to take some lessons from them and alter their preconceived notions about families to reflect current realities.

While the political focus today is on saving marriages and preserving traditional family values, Americans in large numbers are dancing to their own drummers. They're cohabiting in increasingly large numbers, having more children "out of wedlock" and engaging in serial marriages. While the rates of divorce have come down from their 1981 highs, they have leveled off at a high rate that is predicted to remain stable. To meet the needs of children and parents, we need to burst the balloon about idealized families and support families as they really live their lives. And that means we have to face the true complexities of *our* families and not search for simple answers.

As you read this book, keep in mind that we can all look back on our childhoods and note something about our mothers or fathers or sisters or brothers that has had lasting effects on our personalities. If you are looking to answer the question of whether a parental divorce results in children having more or less problems than children who grew up in other living situations, you will be disappointed. Nor will you find answers to whether the stresses of divorce are worse for children than other stresses in life. However, you will find answers here to questions about how and why individual children respond in different ways to the variations in their divorced families.

Divorce is a stressful life event that requires increased focus on parenting. The effort and care that parents put into establishing their postdivorce families are crucial and will pay off over the years in their many benefits to the children. But remember, families are complex, and if you find easy answers, they are likely to be wrong.

Chapter 2

THE ADULT CHILDREN
SPEAK

The Real Legacy of Divorce

*S*ure, *I would have liked to have had that perfect family that's*
on the cover of every magazine at Christmas. None of my
friends had this perfect family but it's the one that every kid imag-
ines the most popular kid at school has. I was only seven when my
parents separated and I don't really remember much about what
it was like when we all lived together, but I remember feeling sad
and confused when they told me.

My parents were really young when they got married . . . it's
hard for me to even imagine them together. I think the divorce
was a good decision, a necessary one, and I think we're all better
off because of it today. I'm pretty lucky because my mom and dad
told me that no matter what happened between them they both
still loved me . . . I always knew I was very valued. In some ways
I think the divorce made both my parents really emphasize how
much they cared about me. Some friends of mine with married
parents didn't know where they stood in terms of their parents'
affection or felt neglected or had pretty bad living situations.

I'm not saying it was always easy. I remember times when my parents disagreed about some decision that involved me and I felt caught in the middle. Sometimes I felt angry about the scheduling and going back and forth. I remember feeling really jealous when my mom told me her boyfriend Dan was moving in. I was surprised when my dad told me he was getting remarried and I really resented my stepmom and her kids. Now I'm really close with my stepmom and I think she makes a much better mate for my dad than my mom did. I'm also close with my "stepdad," even though he and my mom never married and he's now married to someone else. It's confusing to explain all the relationships, and I used to be embarrassed about it, but now I feel lucky to have four parents. They were all there at my college graduation and I think it's widened my view of what I think a family is . . . it's helped me to communicate better and more freely with people who are important to me.

Sharon is one of the 173 adult children whose stories you will be hearing throughout this book. Twenty years later, her reflections on her history reveal her feelings about how her life has been affected by the changes that followed her parents' divorce. She is one of many of the adults I studied who were products of reasonably good divorces. There were others, however, who felt that their parents' divorce left indelible black marks that couldn't be erased. As they reflected on their lives, their pictures revealed conflictual family relationships and continuing personal distress.

For the majority of the adult children in this study, the effects of their parents' marital and remarital relationships, the personalities of each of their parents and the postdivorce life changes formed a complex quilt of good and bad experiences that made up the fabric of their lives. Certainly the common experience of parental divorce imposed issues and dilemmas in their lives that were not present for children whose parents didn't divorce. But their individual responses revealed unique strengths and vulnerabilities that clearly affected *how they made sense* of what happened. In other words, how they were "affected" by divorce had as much to do with their own unique coping abilities and resources as it did with the event itself.

THE STRESSES AND STRAINS OF NORMAL FAMILIES

I wear a T-shirt with a cartoon showing a large auditorium with a banner across the front reading, "Adult Children of Normal Parents, Annual Convention." The audience consists of only two people. Most of us grew up in families that don't quite match up to our visions of what family life should be like. Maybe Dad worked long hours and was unavailable when we wanted or needed him, or maybe he drank too much or maybe he was too strict with us. Maybe Mom was depressed, or overwhelmed, or too critical of us. Maybe Mom and Dad yelled a lot, or went out all the time, or didn't like each other very much. Regardless of their parents' marital status, all children experience stressful life events that require them to be resourceful and activate their coping abilities.

It is a rare child—of any age—who doesn't find his or her parents' divorce distressing. Studies that focus on children of divorce during the crisis stage, the first two years afterward, report that a majority feel angry, sad and depressed. Most feel confused and anxious about what losses the separation will bring. As we read about these findings we tend to conclude that the pain children feel when their parents separate is unlike—and greater than—the pain of children who didn't experience a parental divorce.

Most children, however, experience stress and varying degrees of trauma in their growing-up years—the death of a parent, a serious illness in the family, an alcoholic or mentally ill parent, emotional or physical abuse, or poverty. Ask me to reflect on what I felt living with my parents' "intact" high-conflict marriage of fifty years or ask my cousin Barbara about her feelings about the death of her father when she was eleven, or my friend Ethelyn, who grew up with a mentally ill mother, or my friend Sue, whose younger sister drowned while in Sue's care. Ask any of us to talk about the feelings we had about these unhappy circumstances, and you will tap feelings of sadness, loss, anxiety and the pain of coping with difficult family stressors. Ask us if these circumstances affected who we are as adults today, and you'll get a resounding yes.

THE IMPACT OF CHILDHOOD STRESS

How any of these early experiences influenced each of us varies greatly. We may feel a pervasive sense of sadness, or we may feel grateful that we have survived as well as we have. How stressors impact children depends on such factors as whether they are prolonged or brief, whether it is a single event or a series of cumulative experiences. It also depends on whether children have learned adequate coping resources and have other factors in their lives that can protect them from succumbing to the stressors.

As adults, when we examine our lives, trying to figure out why we feel certain ways, or why we feel stuck, or why we can't find the mate we want, we look to what therapists call our "family of origin" to figure out why we are who we are. Do I keep choosing partners who are critical of me because my mother was often critical of me and it feels familiar? Am I having trouble staying with a job for more than a year because my father held one job all his life and complained about it daily? Do I crave excitement because my family was always chaotic and that's what I got used to? We may blame our histories for our lack of achievement as adults, or we may attribute our achievements to overcoming our family traumas. We may come to accept the imperfections of our parents and even hold them in high regard, knowing that they did the best they could do, given their own histories.

Although I do not want to minimize the potential long-term effects of a parental divorce, I think it is a mistake to exaggerate its negative impact, because it causes us to distort the realities. There is no doubt that a parental divorce temporarily upsets the equilibrium of children's lives, but we also know that it is our *perception* of a life event that influences our reaction.

THE STUDY

Before I discuss the findings, let me give you some background about the study. This book is based on the fourth stage of the Binuclear Family Study, a landmark twenty-year study of family relationships after divorce. This research is the first long-term study of divorce to

- use a random sampling method
- focus on a broad range of divorced families
- include parents, children and stepparents in one study.

Two decades ago, after reading study after study that focused only on the problems of children due to divorce, I wanted to respond to the many parents and their children who over and over again asked me for a more balanced view.

I began the study with interviews of ninety-eight pairs of parents who had been legally divorced for one year. During these initial interviews I became acutely aware of how the divorce was just a starting point for the complex family lives that were to follow. Most of the parents had been separated for at least a year prior to their legal divorce and many had formed new intimate relationships with adults who had become part of their children's lives. Clearly, to get a true picture of these families, I needed to interview these new significant partners. Two years after the initial interviews with the divorced parents, and then again two years later, the parents were interviewed along with their cohabiting and remarriage partners. These three interviews, conducted over five years, included 256 people in all, and revealed how divorce rearranged their families. The complexities and nuances of the transitions that led to these changes were the subject of my earlier book, *The Good Divorce*.

At the twenty-year mark, I decided once again to revisit these families. This time I chose to interview their children, all of whom were now twenty-one years old or older. They lived all over the country and locating them was a long and difficult process that took over a year. Much to my surprise, however, we found all but eleven of them. Once they heard we had interviewed their parents and stepparents several times, they were eager to participate. They wanted their views to be heard.

Studies on other topics found telephone interviews to be as reliable and valid as in-person interviews and much more feasible with a large group of geographically distant individuals. Using this approach, 173 adult children from 89 of the original 98 families were interviewed. Their interviews were tape-recorded and then transcribed, so that written and audio versions of each and every individual interview were available to me.

I then received a fellowship to the Radcliffe Institute for Advanced Studies at Harvard to spend the next year analyzing the vast amount of data from these interviews (see the appendix for a more complete description of the study).

Who They Are

The average age now of the almost equal number of males and females is thirty-one years old. Primarily middle class, over half have completed college and are employed as professionals. At the time of their parents' divorce almost half were in their middle childhood years, one-fifth were preschoolers, one-quarter were in early adolescence and the rest were in late adolescence or young adulthood.

Slightly over half have married (ninety) and 29 percent of those who had married have divorced. Of the twenty-six adults who had divorced, one-third have remarried. Two-fifths of the whole sample have children, and their average age at the birth of their first child was twenty-seven. The average age at which they had married (twenty-five), their age at the time of the birth of their first child, and the percent who had divorced are similar to other adults in their age range, regardless of family structure.

Of those who were single at the time of our interview, slightly over half are currently in serious relationships and half of this group lived with their partners. That leaves about one-quarter who were not involved in a serious intimate relationship when we interviewed them, although many talked about having recently ended a relationship. Only a few said that they had never experienced a serious involvement.

When Complexity Is Normal

One striking similarity that makes these adult children different from their peers with married parents is that almost all of them had to adapt to complex family situations. Over the twenty years since their parents divorced, almost all of them had experienced multiple changes in family composition, as most of their parents dated, cohabited, remarried and some redivorced.

During the course of their childhoods, almost all of them gained stepparents. It is notable that of the eighty-nine families, it is in only four that neither parent remarried. In addition to the remarriages, many noted that their parents had other serious relationships, some cohabiting, either before their remarriages or after a second divorce. Many of them formed relationships with their parents' "intimate others." Some lasted well into adulthood, others dissolved. One-quarter of their remarried mothers and fathers had experienced a second divorce.

Having four parents was not unusual and almost two-thirds (63 percent) had both stepmothers and stepfathers. And having stepparents usually meant having new siblings. One hundred and twenty-four adult children—72 percent of the total group—gained at least one stepsibling as a result of either their mothers' or their fathers' remarriages. Some step relationships were good; others were bad. Some were short term and others more permanent. Although less common than stepsiblings, almost one-fifth also gained half siblings. As we shall see in chapter 6, how they reacted to their stepparents and new siblings—and how these relationships developed and changed—varied greatly.

Challenging the Stereotypes

It is clear as day that for the great majority of these adult children, divorce, while clearly difficult, has not doomed their lives. In psychological terms, they are developmentally on target. Comparing themselves to other people they know, most rate themselves as average or above average on self-esteem, success and overall happiness. The immediate distress surrounding parental separation usually faded with time and most of the children settled into a pattern of normal development. Although they went through difficult times and experienced stressful family changes, most emerged stronger and wiser in spite of—or perhaps because of—their complex histories.

It is their memories, insights and emotions that determine the lens through which they view life, and the lens through which they will view divorce. And so it is with all of us. When I was growing up, for example, I remember feeling that I was my father's favorite child. It doesn't matter if my father felt he had no favorites among his children, or if my brother thinks he was my father's favorite. The fact is that I have gone through life feeling affirmed by "knowing" that I was my father's special child. As with all of us, the events of the lives of these adults are defined and transformed through their personal filters. No two stories are alike and siblings surprised me with their divergent memories and reactions, teaching me once again how our perceptions become the "facts" we live by.

What I was not prepared for, however, was the striking direction of the findings because they clearly and boldly contradict our deeply entrenched stereotypes that children remain angry and bitter about their parents' divorces. Quite the opposite. What I found was that the majority of these young adults were very clear that their parents' divorces had positive outcomes, not only for their parents but for themselves as well. A few statistics from my study speak volumes about the real legacy of divorce in children's lives. Of 173 adult children of divorce:

- 76 percent do *not* wish their parents were still together
- 79 percent feel their parents' decision to divorce was a good one
- 79 percent feel that their parents are better off today
- 78 percent feel that *they* are either better off or not affected

Making Sense of Their Family Histories

During our intensive interviews we asked questions such as, "Do you think the divorce made you different from your friends whose parents did not get a divorce?" and "How did you feel about growing up in a divorced family?" The participants answered these questions easily. But when we then asked how they thought the divorce *improved* their lives, most were surprised by the question. They had not been asked that question before and they had to take some time to think about it.

The ways in which we understand our lives are influenced by the broader stories of our culture. Given the negative societal images of divorce, it should be no surprise that it was much easier for our participants to tell us about the negative effects of divorce. Narrative therapy, a mode of psychotherapy that has been gaining in popularity over the past decade, offers some insights about how we use our histories to figure out why we are who we are. It is based on the notion that the stories that shape our lives are culturally framed.

The narrative school of thought teaches that by challenging fixed and pessimistic versions of life events, new and more optimistic stories can be envisioned. Their approach to therapy is to help people "re-author" their lives by developing healthier interpretations of their life experiences. " As people step back and separate from the problem and then consider its history and negative effects, they can find themselves standing in a different territory than the one they have become used to. This different territory is often a place free from practices such as self-blame and judgment."

As I pointed out in the last chapter, most of what we know about the effects of divorce focuses on problems. Not wanting to ignore the negative fallouts from divorce, I asked them many questions that were asked in other studies of divorce. However, because I also wanted to know if there were gains as well as losses related to their parents' divorces, I specially framed questions to reveal both sides of the coin, such as, "Do you think you are better or worse off or unaffected by your parents' divorce?" and "Are there some ways in which the divorce improved your life?"

Turning the tables in this way enabled these adult children to look at their histories in a new way. It resulted in a range of mixed feelings that better represent the complexities and ambiguities that most of us feel when we reflect on our histories. Like most other young adults, they had concerns about repeating dysfunctional patterns from their families of origin. Their parents' personalities, behaviors and lifestyles came under close scrutiny as they sized up what they liked and what they didn't. The interpersonal issues mentioned over and over were *commitment, trust,* and *dealing with conflict.* On a personal level, they spoke about *independence* and *resilience.* These issues are precisely the ones that most adults in this stage of their development grapple with, whether they grow up in a nuclear family or not.

On Commitment

Commitment is one of those highly overused words that has many different meanings. When it comes to relationships, commitment usually takes some form of promising or giving one's word to another person about your dedicated plans of giving yourself to and staying in the relationship. "Till death do us part" wedding vows are heard less frequently now than they were a generation ago, and couples instead write individually designed vows of commitment, often based on their beliefs about marriage, divorce and individual freedoms. These changes in wedding vows suggest that this generation is less likely to want to make a commitment for "as long as we both shall live," less likely to commit to the *institution* of marriage, and more likely to commit to the *process* of working on the relationship.

Recently, however, in reaction to the three decades of high divorce rates, religious conservatives are promoting "covenant marriage" laws and policies, calling for the return of the everlasting commitment vows. Interestingly, the couples who divorced in the late 1970s and early 1980s—the parents of the adults in this study—did so during the peak of the divorce rates and they were also the couples who took those traditional "till death do us part" vows when they married. The covenant marriage vows are similar to those of the past generations, but the new versions expand to exclude unilateral divorces and include premarital and reconciliation counseling intended to ward off divorce. Most of this generation appears unwilling, however, to return to everlasting commitment vows, and, in a clear disappointment to those promoting them, covenant marriage laws are not sweeping the nation.

However, despite changing vows, it is still a rare person who enters marriage expecting that he or she will divorce. Patterns of marriage and divorce may be changing, but evidence suggests that many of our attitudes and beliefs about marriage have changed little over the recent past. Most Americans believe that marriage is a lifetime relationship and should only be ended in extreme circumstances. One exception to this is short-term marriages that don't include children. When there are no children involved, some have proposed the notion that these are really trial marriages or "starter marriages," because they can be easily terminated without stigma.

The difference between children of divorce and their contemporaries who didn't experience a parental divorce is simply that those who witnessed their parents' divorce know firsthand that marriage isn't always forever. But this certainly didn't mean that they take marriage any less seriously. In fact, most of those I studied valued marriage highly, and because they did, they were cautious about rushing into it.

Kevin was fourteen when his parents separated after twenty years of marriage. He was "crushed" and angry at the time and after a difficult adolescence, including some heavy alcohol and drug use for most of his high school years, he then completed college and graduate school and has a successful career. At twenty-five he married, and now, ten years after his marriage, he reflects on a silver lining in his parents' divorce.

I am sure that the strength of my marriage today is due to the fact that I had a front-row seat of what not to do. My parents had decided to get married after six weeks, whereas my wife and I had known each other a number of years, and were close friends for a while, and then moved halfway across the country together before deciding to get married. I know I was a lot more cognizant of my own relationship and what I wanted, and didn't want, to happen, so it probably made me a better spouse. . . . To be honest, I wouldn't want to go through a divorce and because of that I know that I am going to do everything in my power to not have that happen. So, it has changed my relationship with significant others for the better—absolutely for the better.

Brian was only five when his parents split up. Although honest about the divorce's negative effects, he feels that it also helped him become more independent and better equipped in his intimate relationships. He is in a cohabiting relationship, has no immediate plans for marriage and, like Kevin, feels that marriage is a very important decision.

In general, I think it has had very positive effects. I see what happens in divorces, and I have promised myself that I would do anything to not get a divorce. I don't want my kids to go through what I went through. I also think I have learned that communication is very important, and that it is important to really take a long time to think about and make sure that this is the person who I want to and can spend the rest of my life with.

Tracy, a married mother of two, was twelve when her parents divorced. Although she resented the divorce because she was "very family oriented and . . . old-fashioned," she feels she learned from their marital relationship how not to repeat their mistakes.

> I saw some of the things that my parents did and know not to do that in my marriage and see the way that they treated each other and know not to do that to my spouse and my children. I know it's made me more committed to my husband and my children.

Like Kevin, Brian and Tracy, most of the young adults I studied felt that divorce was a painful experience, and as adults they felt strongly that they did not want to repeat their parents' histories. Even though as adults they feel the divorce taught them important lessons, divorce was not viewed as an easy exit from a failing marriage.

Others remain wary of commitment. Amanda was ten when her parents legally divorced, although they had separated seven years earlier when she was only three. Now, thirty and single, she has a successful and fulfilling career, good relationships with her parents and stepparents, and many close friends.

> That is the question of the hour. I've had two or three significant relationships and I haven't really felt ready to commit to anyone yet so it's starting to occur to me—I start to wonder if I'll actually be able to commit to somebody or if maybe because I never saw a committed relationship last in my parental figures if maybe I don't have a model for that. Although now my dad and Gwen have been married for a long time, I sometimes wonder if that is subconsciously affecting some of my decisions.

As she reflected further on commitment, Amanda realized that her views of marriage were connected to her issues with commitment. "I think I am more tentative about marriage than some of my friends whose parents were married all through their childhood. To me, it seems so overwhelming and so much work to make a good marriage but it seems more feasible to them."

Todd, seven when his parents divorced, is single and not currently involved in a serious relationship. He thinks the divorce benefited him in some ways and thinks he is a more caring and understanding person because of it. He feels it broadened his views of life and notes that he admires his stepfather and has a good relationship with him. But he also notes that the divorce has been harmful in terms of his intimate relationships.

> I don't want to admit this but it is probably the most significant reason why I am twenty-seven years old and the longest relationship I've had with anyone is ten months. If I can reach a year anniversary with anyone, I will be doing backflips!

Adam, age nine at the time of his parents' divorce, is single and living with his girlfriend of two years. Both of his parents remarried and then had a second divorce, which he thinks may have affected how he feels about marriage.

> If you ask my friends, they would say I'm afraid to get married. I don't know if it's based on the divorce or just the way I think. I don't think my relationship with significant others is impacted hugely. But I think any marriage that lasts more than ten years is a milestone. I would say I don't look at marriage as being one of the greatest institutions in the world.

While a parent's marriage and/or divorce may impact how young adults feel about commitment, some sociologists suggest that the lack of commitment during one's twenties is a current social trend. It goes hand in hand with increased education, which in turn has led to delaying marriage. On average, the young adults in our study were more highly educated than their parents, live more independent lifestyles and are part of a generation that is marrying at least five years later than their parents did. Especially for the young women in our study, the social differences between their mothers' generation and their own are quite pronounced. Two examples of this are the social acceptance of cohabitation and having children "out of wedlock." While some of their mothers married because they were pregnant, none of the young adult women felt this same pressure to marry.

On Trust

Trust, or lack of it, was also a common issue for many of the children of divorce as they talked about how they felt about commitment. Trust is closely linked with what we believe about the reliability of others. Research about trust issues after divorce shows inconsistent findings, but in a recent study it was found that when young adults with divorced parents were compared to those with married parents, no differences were found in their trust levels. What was found, however, is that the most influential factors in trusting intimates are early relationships with parents and contemporary experiences with romantic relationships and marriage.

These two influential factors appeared over and over again as the participants talked about their feelings and concerns about trust. If as children they were distrustful of their mothers or fathers, they were likely to be distrustful of relationships in their own lives.

Carole, recently marred at age thirty-one, felt her lack of trust in men happened before the divorce.

There's no way I could ever trust men after what my father did. I was ten when they separated but my father and mother had been fighting about the other women in his life for years. After the divorce, it was just my mother and me. I had several relationships before I married Tom and most of them disappointed me. I'm learning to trust Tom, but I must say that I still have a long way to go.

Doug is twenty-nine and single. He noted that his inability to trust women, until recently, wasn't so much about his parents' divorce as it was his relationship with his mother.

I'm surprised most of the time that Erica is still with me after four years. I know that's because of my mother. Even as a little kid, before the divorce, I knew I couldn't trust her. She was a drinker and I never knew what mood she'd be in when I got home, or even if she was going to be there. I'm always testing Erica's love and she keeps telling me that she'll be there for me . . . and she is. She teases me because every day I become a little more trusting and share something else with her. I'm much more open now than I was before I met her.

Changes in relationships with both parents are likely to occur as parents establish new intimate relationships in their own lives. One of the major risks that divorce presents is the possibility of a loss of relationship between children and their fathers. This possibility is most likely to occur when mothers have sole custody. Those adults who saw less of their fathers after divorce, or whose fathers abandoned them, traced their distrustful feelings to their fathers' betrayal of their mothers or themselves. For some of the women in our study this was a major negative impact of divorce. As we will see in chapter 5, for many, it is the relationships with their fathers that became the most vulnerable after divorce.

On Resolving Conflicts

It practically goes without saying that as a group, these kids experienced some degree of conflict between their parents, either when they were married or after the divorce. Some weren't privy to arguments, while others were exposed to constant bickering and fighting. In either of these extremes, children had no role models for healthy problem solving in intimate relationships. However, although they may not have had their parents as role models, many did see their parents in remarriages that were better and learned positive ways of resolving conflict from these second marriages. Others turned to friends' parents and sought counseling to help them cope more effectively with conflict.

Children who live in abusive, high-conflict family situations, irrespective of whether their parents are married or divorced, have good reason to fear conflict. They learn the real dangers of how conflicts can escalate and often are fearful at the first sign of raised voices. As adults, many avoid conflict to the point that they are unable to resolve minor differences that are a normal part of intimate relationships.

Some, like Wendy, who was fourteen at the time of her parents' separation, painfully remember their parents' frequent conflicts. In Wendy's case, her parents' fights often came very close to becoming physical. Married for the second time after divorcing a man who was abusive to her, she feels this marriage is good but she worries that her fears about conflict will have a negative effect.

> I have a real fear of conflict so I try to avoid conflict by holding things in, and then I just stew. I just shut up, instead of expressing myself, for fear that things will just explode. I hate conflict, and I know this is related to all the conflict in my parents' marriage as well as their divorce.

Angela, twenty-nine and single, had a very different experience with conflict. She only remembers her parents having one loud argument that was followed by her father moving out. Even though she was just nine, this episode marking the end of the marriage left an indelible impression:

> . . . my parents didn't argue or fight in front of us kids, I witnessed that one fight, and so in relationships it was very difficult for me. Over time it got better, but if I got into an argument, it was like, Oh, my God, is it done? I know that the marriage didn't end from that one argument, but still, as a kid, that's what locked into my head. It's one of the last things I remember of them being married. No matter how far or deep you bury that, it keeps coming forth.

Michael was seven when his parents divorced, but only three when they separated, and he has no memory of them being together. For the first four or five years after the divorce, his parents had frequent arguments and he often felt caught in the middle. He feels that the divorce has taught him to be more adaptable, but he also feels that it has had a negative effect on his intimate relationships. Twenty-seven now, he is single and not currently in a relationship.

> I can't separate myself from it—I mean I can't parcel myself out to say which piece of who I am is because of the divorce. It has impacted me, and shaped who I am. I think I approach relationships with that looming over me— when it comes to relationships with women, then I can feel how much it impacts me. It looms over me in my relationships—I've had girlfriends tell me that I am argumentative, and I think that my parents and seeing them argue is a part of this.

A quick scan of the available self-help books shows that resolving conflicts is probably more popular than almost any other topic, although commitment and trust certainly compete for second place. How to negotiate, how to fight fairly, how to listen well, how to be intimate all deal in some way with how to resolve differences. The good news is that all these are skills that can be learned.

Fears of commitment are linked to trust and it's rare for someone to reach adulthood without having experienced being hurt and disappointed by someone you gave your trust to. When these experiences were devastatingly traumatic, like early abandonment or abuse by a parent, the wounds are deep and long lasting. A small minority of the adults in this study suffered these kinds of traumas and as adults were very fearful of dependency and intimacy. But for the majority, although they identified these issues as tied to the divorce of their parents, they were forming intimate relationships much in the same way as their contemporaries were.

Other Effects, Both Beneficial and Destructive

In addition to their comments about the effect of divorce on their behavior in intimate relationships and their attitudes toward divorce and remarriage, the adult children talked about many other ways—both beneficial and destructive—that divorce impacted them. Many talked about the ways that divorce made them stronger and more independent as adults. For some like Doris, this was because the divorce was a painful and sometimes traumatizing experience that caused soul-searching and forced them to learn how to cope. "I think that living through difficult childhood situations forces you to figure out why your own life is such a mess . . . and then you either work hard to overcome it, or go in the downward spiral."

Andy, age thirty-two, talks about the value of becoming more independent.

> I learned a lot. I grew up a lot more quickly than a lot of my friends. Not that that's a good thing or a bad thing. People were always thinking I was older than I was because of the way I carried myself. And I think that was good to be involved with people and learn about relationships. It taught me a lot. I think in that way it was beneficial.

Tim, age twenty-five, notes that he feels the divorce had a positive impact on him that resulted in improved relationship skills.

> I think it's made me value relationships and friendships. I think it's helped me to become a more critical thinker and to communicate better and more freely with people who are important to me. I don't really take relationships for granted. I know that you have to work at them to make them viable. I think in other ways it's made me more independent—I did a lot of traveling in planes alone when I was young. I kind of had to learn to express myself coherently at a relatively young age about what I wanted and what was making me mad, what a reasonable demand was and that kind of thing. I think it's really shaped my personality a lot.

Others noted how it remedied a dysfunctional family situation. When a child experiences the chronic stress of parental conflict, the divorce can provide relief.

> I think relieving tension was the main one. Just taking away that tension I felt like it enabled me to grow up a little easier. I suspect if they hadn't gotten divorced I would

not have had as good a relationship during those years with either of my parents.

Another source of beneficial effects was related to the new family members they gained over the years.

It's made a big difference in my life—how could it not? I think it has really shaped me. I have extra parental support—especially from my stepmom, who is one of my best friends, and I have a little sister, who is also one of my best friends.

I got a great little sister! Both my parents are happy, and my father is clean and sober.

I have such a large family since the divorce. I can't imagine my life without all of them. I'm really glad I got to know and be around people who love me!

Scars That Didn't Heal

A full 20 percent of the respondents felt that their parents' marriage, the divorce, and the postdivorce family combined to have a devastating impact, leaving emotional scars that didn't heal. They blamed their parents for their own difficulties and failures in intimate relationships as well as for other failures and disappointments in their lives.

Nicole, the younger of two children, was nine when her parents separated. She's single, living with her boyfriend and her two children by two previous relationships. Even though she thinks she is better off because of her parents' divorce and would have been "pretty messed up" if they had stayed together, she feels the divorce "ripped her apart."

I don't trust. I don't get close. I am afraid to get married. I am afraid of being abandoned, and that I am not going to be good enough. I'm afraid that I will be married for five years or whatever, and he'll walk out on me. It has really impacted me in a major way—it is such a big amount, probably more than 75 percent of who I am is because of the divorce. It has made me who I am.

Among those who felt that the divorce was detrimental, there were some strikingly similar family histories. The majority grew up in high-conflict families, both pre- and postdivorce. Many noted their parents' alcohol or physical abuse, or both, and many had at least one parent who had serious psychological problems.

Even though this group of adults felt strongly that the divorce had been detrimental, for some the dark cloud had a silver lining. They were determined not to repeat the mistakes their parents had made. For example, Patricia, now thirty-three, who is divorced herself, has an amicable relationship with her ex because of what she learned from her parents, who remain fiery foes to this day. She had this to say:

The way I raise my children—the way I love, and treat my children, especially in my own divorce. I will not fight with their father over my two kids. I refuse to. So, I learned a lot from their divorce.

It was in this group in particular that siblings had the most extreme differences in their reactions and coping abilities. They often differed markedly in how they responded to the hand they were dealt. It was not unusual to find one child in the family who felt successful in his or her life while another felt badly damaged. Some were highly resilient and overcame unstable and sometimes devastating family histories, while others were still suffering great pain or anger. It's important for us to remember that not all children in a family are treated equally, nor do they have the same individual capacities to bounce back from dysfunctional family situations.

In chapter 8 we will see how such factors as age, birth order, gender and individual temperaments interacted with parental relationships to result in different experiences and reactions from children who grew up in the same family.

SO, WHAT CAN WE DO?

As parents, and as adult children, we need to understand that parents can't change their children's temperaments and other inherited qualities; what they can do is support their children in the very way parents live their lives and relate to their kids. Life is full of hard knocks and parents can either act as buffers, or protective influences, or they can add to the risk of their children's emotional pain and distress. Family relationships have the potential to mediate the effects that both genetics and environmental factors have on children's development. The reverse is also true: Genetics and environmental factors can mediate the effects of destructive family relationships.

Once again, a reminder before we attempt to peel away the next layer of this complex question: There are no easy, sound bite answers that explain the effects of divorce on any one child. It is in the unique combining of genetic and environmental history that we discover the true picture of the meaning that individual children attribute to divorce. It is not the fact of divorce, nor whether their parents divorced or stayed married that tells the story. It is the emotional quality of the relationships within that family along with the individual personalities of each parent and child that combine with other environmental factors to produce a whole.

Chapter 3

LINGERING MEMORIES ABOUT THEIR PREDIVORCE FAMILY

Adult Children Look Back at Their Parents'
Marriages Before the Divorce

O ne day, after teaching a graduate seminar in divorce and remarriage, I was approached at my office door by one of my students. She was obviously upset. "Why didn't you say any-thing about the crappy stuff that goes on in families before the divorce? Everything always gets blamed on the divorce, but that's only the half of it. Let me tell you, most of the scars I have hap-pened way before that." Julia continued softly, her eyes filling with tears. "My family was a mess. My father drank too much and when he came home drunk there was hell to pay for all of us. I can remember how scared my sister and I were. We used to sneak upstairs and hide under the bed and cover our ears with our pillows. The rest of the time my mother was depressed and didn't get out of bed most of the day. I was so ashamed of my house I never brought a friend home. The damage was already done by the time my father finally left."

Of course, she was right. But at that time there was no research about children and divorce that included the child's pre-divorce family history, and I wasn't prepared to speak about it. Even today, rarely does the parents' marital relationship get mentioned in discussions of the effects of divorce on children. It's almost as if everything in the marriage is going along fine and then, whammo, out of the blue, one day there's a divorce. Julia knew better.

THE IMPACT OF
THE PREDIVORCE FAMILY

The idea that we can look at the effects of divorce without looking also at family life before divorce denies the reality: Spouses who are happily married don't divorce. Divorces are preceded by troubled marriages and troubled marriages affect a child's development as well as the quality of family life and parent-child relationships. In fact, many of children's problems that are attributed to divorce are actually rooted in their parents' marriage.

If you are already divorced, you may be wondering, "Okay, but that's all in the past. How is knowing that my troubled marriage is a contributing factor going to help me now? How is it going to reduce my children's suffering or distress now that I'm divorced?" While of course it's true that you can't go back and change the dynamics of your marriage, you can better understand how it affected your children's reactions to your divorce. If one of your children is having problems that have been attributed to the divorce, you will be better able to sort out the true origins of her problems, thus helping your child to better understand why she is feeling the way she does.

You may also find relief in knowing that even if you weren't able to reduce the negative impact of your marriage on your children, you may indeed have made a wise choice to improve your children's lives by leaving your marriage.

Of course one's predivorce family can have positive as well as negative effects. How well the parents meet a child's needs for nurturance and security, how well the marriage provides an environment in which children can grow and flourish, how well a child's developmental needs are met—all these factors will set the stage for a child's reaction to a marital separation.

Age makes a difference here, too. Given that older siblings simply clock more time in the predivorce family than younger ones, it follows that the predivorce family will have a greater impact on them. In contrast, younger siblings who spend fewer years living with their married parents are likely to be more influenced by the living situations after the divorce. It is no surprise, then, that studies that try to determine whether divorce is worse for younger or older children end up with inconsistent findings. In other words, perhaps it's not just a developmental issue so much as a matter of length of exposure to different household environments. There are simply too many factors that need to be accounted for before any reliable conclusions can be drawn.

In a highly dysfunctional marriage, for example, parents' energies are often so absorbed by their marital problems that their capacity to parent well is diminished. In a less dysfunctional marriage, like the good-enough or devitalized marriages I will describe in a moment, the fact that many parents are less invested in their marriages often means that they divert more of their need for closeness to their children. It only follows that if parents' daily lives are not consumed by their marital distress they are freer emotionally to be involved as parents, more available to meet their children's needs, which may lessen the negative impact of the marriage on the child's experience of the divorce. Even in the best of situations, however, when a divorce is imminent, parents' capacities for parenting may be temporarily reduced. As we will see in Part II, two important factors that can either mitigate or exacerbate some of the stresses, not only of the separation itself but also of the lingering effects of the marriage, are the way parents relate to each other and to their children after the divorce.

Different Ages, Different Memories

Adults who were younger than seven when their parents divorced usually remember very little, if anything, of their parents' married life. Alan, who was not quite four when his parents separated, is typical.

> I mean, I know they were married, and I've seen pictures, but I don't have any memory of how they were together. I can't even imagine them together in one house. This way seems normal to me because it's the way it's always been. My mom and dad live in separate houses and I spend time with both of them.

Like Alan, younger children's knowledge of their parents' marriage usually comes from photos or stories told to them by siblings, parents or grandparents.

Although children between the ages of seven and eleven will often carry significant memories of their parents' marriages into adulthood, it is usually the children who are eleven or older who are the most deeply affected because they spent the longest period of time living in the predivorce family. As we shall see throughout the book, siblings often hold different perceptions of their parents' marriage and divorce. Age, gender, birth order, temperament and individual relationships with each parent will all impact their memories of their parents' marriage. These memories are indelibly imprinted, providing a lens that they continue to look through as they question the impact of their parents' divorce.

IT DOESN'T JUST HAPPEN

Needless to say, divorce doesn't just happen. Something about the marriage is unsatisfying, whether to one or both partners and, usually after a lot of soul-searching, the unhappiness peaks and someone initiates a breakup. Of course not all spouses who divorce have loud, screaming fights or are physically abusive with each other. According to current studies, between one-third and one-half of marriages that ended in divorce had serious unresolved conflicts that resulted in frequent heated arguments like the ones described by my student Julia in the story that opened this chapter. That leaves at least half of failed marriages that don't fit our warring stereotype but nevertheless were bad enough to cause at least one of the partners to make the painful, life-changing decision to divorce.

Most adult children remember both the good and the bad times. Those whose parents had prolonged conflict won't have many happy memories, while others will hold memories of occasional happy moments. Some won't remember seeing any affection between their parents, while others, especially those who were older at the time of divorce, may remember affectionate times between their parents, especially during the early years in the marriage.

In the best-case scenarios, children after divorce continue to integrate pleasant childhood memories of the predivorce family into their adult lives. Enduring memories of happy times are shared with friends, siblings, parents and grandparents. In spite of the divorce, the predivorce family still provides a solid foundation in their current lives.

In the worst-case scenarios, it is clear that even into adulthood, the deep pain and anger children felt about their family life before the divorce still persists. For many, their parents' marriages had a far greater impact on them than their divorces. For some, the divorce actually provided relief from the stress. Unfortunately, for others, it did not.

Most adult children will differentiate between conflicts that surfaced in the year just prior to the separation and those that endured for many years. Although stressful in the short term, brief situational conflict usually doesn't have long-term consequences. In fact, when overt conflict is present only in the year prior to the divorce, children will tend to remember their parents' marriage as mostly happy. These good memories of their family life become integrated into their history. Pleasant memories from our childhood help build our self-confidence and esteem. Even though their parents eventually divorced, it doesn't erase the positive effects of happier times.

THE THREE TYPES OF MARRIAGES

Back in the 1970s, when I first started this research, I found that most marriages that end in divorce can be characterized as either good enough, devitalized, or high conflict.

Good-enough Marriages

Good-enough marriages are just that: good enough to meet the needs of the children. These marriages are not necessarily without problems or conflicts, but the problems don't disrupt the family relationships or interfere with parenting.

These are the couples that set outsiders to wondering what could be the reasons for the divorce. As a couple, they may share little intimacy but, for the most part, they act respectfully toward one another. If there is anger between them, it usually doesn't escalate into serious conflicts. Child-focused, they manage to compartmentalize their marital issues so that they don't intrude on the emotional climate of their children's everyday lives. From the children's point of view, their parents seem to get along quite amicably—that is, until shortly before the divorce.

Matt was ten years old at the time of his parents' divorce. Now thirty-one, he is married with two children of his own. He spoke for many others in this group: "I never had any idea there were any problems. I thought we were just a normal family. I only remember one time when they were yelling at each other. I can't remember what it was about, but then a few weeks later they told us they were getting a divorce."

If your marriage was good enough, chances are that your children didn't see the divorce coming. Most kids from good-enough marriages express real surprise, shock and confusion when they are told that their parents are divorcing. Cathy, thirteen years old at the time, described feeling shocked at first, and then angry. "I never expected it, not even a hint. I only remember a fight they had that was pretty scary, something about my dad being gone over the weekend. After they split I kept thinking that they were going to get over it and get back together, and then I got angry when they didn't."

Stephen was a teenager with two younger sisters when his parents divorced. His parents, both professionals, met in college and were married for eighteen years. "It just seemed to change overnight. One day they were laughing and the next they were yelling. Then Dad moved out. I kept asking 'why,' and I got different answers from each of them. My mother was furious and said my father was irresponsible."

Stephen's sister was twelve at the time and expressed her confusion. "I just remember being confused. I didn't understand it. It was a bombshell. We kids had no idea it was coming. It just fell out of the clear blue sky. I worried about having to move, to leave my friends . . . and I remember feeling ashamed and embarrassed. I was really sad about it for years."

One myth about divorce that we hold dear is that it is not as distressing to adult children. We assume that when children are eighteen or older, they are less dependent on and have less need for their families. Dana, the oldest of four children, was twenty-four when her parents divorced. She challenges that myth: "I was very upset because I felt that they had made it for twenty-five years and why couldn't they make it any longer than that? I mean, that's a lot of years to invest in someone. And my initial reaction was that our childhood, which I considered at that time a pretty happy childhood, was a sham! So I felt kind of put off base at that point . . . like what is real and what is not real? You have to understand, I was twenty-four at the time, married with two kids and lived a thousand miles away. And still it hit me very hard." The distress expressed by Dana and some of the other older siblings in the study simply contradicts the idea that older children somehow avoid the stresses of divorce.

Although the children of good-enough marriages will no doubt be distressed by their parents' divorces, two major buffers can reduce the potential risks over the long term. First, these were usually child-centered families in which the parents were actively interested, concerned and nurturing. Children who have their developmental needs met and whose childhoods are primarily happy tend to be fairly resilient in the face of divorce.

Second, most good-enough spouses will continue to focus on their children's needs after the divorce, and children can count on fairly uninterrupted relationships with their parents and some kind of shared parenting arrangement postdivorce. A small minority of good-enough parents will go through a period of hostility and anger during the early stages of the divorce, but after a year or two, most will settle down to less acrimonious relationships.

Even though these parents have a time when conflict increases, their history as good parents makes it unlikely that they will involve the children in their disputes. It's important to remember though that not all conflict is bad for children. It becomes destructive to children when parents involve them in the disputes or when it pervades their daily lives and threatens their needs for safety.

Devitalized Marriages

Unlike good-enough marriages, which tend to be fairly amicable and respectful, devitalized marriages tend to be distant, lacking in affection. The couple may have been happy early on, but by the time the children are old enough to register it, the joy has gone out of the marriage. Some couples in devitalized marriages repress their hostilities by seldom engaging with one another, thus creating an atmosphere of cold enmity. One of my clients who was contemplating divorce spoke in a low voice, void of any feelings. "We speak through the children, mainly at meal time. We deal with the necessities of everyday life, but barely talk directly to one another. He's been sleeping in his office downstairs for years now." I asked her how long in her eighteen-year marriage they had lived this way. "I've stopped counting, but it's at least eight or nine years. We were never well suited. We gave up on arguing years ago."

Still other spouses will appear to get along, while one partner is miserable and secretly planning to leave "when the time is right."

Jill was a teenager when her parents divorced. She told us that her mother made it clear in the family that open conflict was to be avoided at all costs. She knew her parents weren't close, but she had no idea that her mother was so miserable that she wanted out of the marriage. When her mother asked her father for a divorce, everyone was shocked. Yes, her mother had been depressed on and off for years, and yes, her mother often went out alone in the evenings, but no one expected divorce.

It wasn't until I was twenty-five and engaged that my mother told me, how, for many years, she felt no love for my dad, and felt very lonely living with him. I was really surprised when she said that she had been thinking about leaving him for almost ten years, but wanted to wait until my sister and I finished high school. Then, tearfully, she apologized. She wished she could have lasted another five years, she said, but she just couldn't live that way any longer. Although I didn't see it back then, I now understand what she was feeling. I love them both, but they're polar opposites. I never understood why they got married in the first place.

Other devitalized couples either resort to quiet, persistent psychological abuse or silently withdraw. A client recently told me that her husband had refused to have sex with her for the past six years, and looked at her with disdain when she asked why. He came and went as he pleased, never telling her when he would be home or where he was going. At first she argued with him about his behavior, but she eventually coped with her hurt and anger by living her life quite separately from him. I asked her what she thought the children knew. "Oh, they know he's not around much, but I think they figure that's because he works long hours. We still share a bedroom, so they don't think anything much is wrong."

Many spouses, like my client, appear to live ordinary, civilized lives but become more and more estranged over time, or find themselves incompatible in one way or another.

Emily, who was fourteen at the time of her parents' divorce, laughs a little as she talks about their marriage: "They were just two people living in the same house. I don't remember seeing any signs of intimacy or affection. They took turns leaving the house. One night my father went out, the next night my mother did. I can remember hearing occasional brief fights, but they never fought in front of us kids."

Her reaction to the divorce was mixed. "I was surprised and angry. I don't remember any talk about divorce and so it really shocked me. I couldn't understand back then why they just couldn't stay together. Now, of course, I understand how empty it felt to my mother, but back then it just seemed normal."

Tom, now thirty-three, describes how he made sense of his parents' divorce.

> I always felt that they cared about each other a great deal and were more communicative with me than a lot of other kids' parents, yet I never remember them being actually together in the same household. So it became a convenient way for me to explain the situation to myself and to friends—that they loved each other but then situations kept them apart—his job, and then time passed. I think I felt when the divorce finally went through, kind of sad and melancholy, but it also seemed to be normal to me that they weren't together.

Emily and Tom's reactions to their parents' separate lives are fairly typical of kids from devitalized marriages. Most children will say that their parents lives weren't miserable and, in fact, many thought that everything in their house was pretty normal. Not hearing arguments, they assume everything is fine and are surprised when their parents split. It is only years later, as adults themselves, that they will realize that their parents were unhappy.

These devitalized marriages provide a model no child wants to emulate. Aaron's response was a common one. "It seemed fine, but it was all that I knew. I look at it now and if I had what I remember them having, I would not be happy. If that's what I brought to my marriage, that's not what I want. But at the time, it was all I knew. I thought I lived in a happy home."

Some kids will be angry or sad, others will say the divorce "isn't a big deal." Many children in these devitalized marriages are used to spending separate times with each parent and their lives may not change too dramatically after the divorce. In their desires to avoid each other, most devitalized couples choose to spend little time together as a family. Some devote more time and energy to their work and career advancement. Others, however,

turn to their children to fill emotional needs unmet in the marriage. It is not uncommon to see a strong mother-child bond
develop in these families that continues during the divorce and
afterward. But even when a father is absent from his children's
lives because of a bad marital relationship, he often forms a closer
bond with his children afterward. Many men find that they no
longer need to escape into their work, and turn their attention to
having a good relationship with their children.

High-Conflict Marriages

High-conflict marriages are the ones that cause serious distress in
children. The anger between parents in these marriages easily
erupts into frightening shouting matches. When children are
exposed to frequent fighting between their parents (as were
nearly one-third of the children I studied), destructive alliances
often form. Sometimes a parent actually invokes a child's support
but often children get involved because they hope that by being
mediators, they can stop the fights. When they side with one parent against the other this alliance usually results in distressing
loyalty conflicts. Except in the case of serious abuse, children
don't want to have to choose between their parents. When they
find themselves in that position they fear hurting a parent and
losing their love.

In high-conflict relationships threats of violence are common.
Although actual violence may not happen every time a fight
occurs, children become hypersensitive to the cues in an argument and fear an escalation that can end in a serious altercation
between their parents. Children in high-conflict families have
vivid memories of the fear and helplessness they felt during these
times. These are the memories that tend not to fade. Even when
kids don't know what their parents are fighting about, the inten-
sity of the fights leaves its mark. Mark was fourteen when his
parents split. He has vivid memories of his parents' marriage. "It

wasn't good! They were always fighting. Some of my earliest memories are of them arguing with each other and I don't remember it making a whole lot of sense. And that pretty much continued throughout until they were divorced. I don't remember why they were fighting, I just remember loud voices and the screaming. I don't remember feeling surprised and I do remember feeling relieved."

Mark's brother Scott was four years younger and remembers being awakened by loud voices of them arguing and bickering at night. "That was very scary. I still don't like being woken up."

Whether long-term or episodic, violence in families will leave children in a constant state of alert and fear. Violence and substance abuse are usually just symptoms of other psychological problems, and often these problems predate the marriage. The point is that in these situations divorce is often a relief to the children. This response by one twelve-year-old girl was similar to other children in this high-conflict marriage group.

Allison, twelve at the time and now thirty-three, remembers that she was tired of living with her parents' fighting. She says that when they divorced, "I remember thinking, well, it's got to get better now. It can't get any worse. They fought all the time. I thought they should have done this a long time ago. . . . I didn't try to keep my parents together. . . . They didn't have to give me a reason—I knew why they were getting a divorce. It was an unhappy relationship. I wasn't sad . . . mostly I was just relieved."

Alcohol abuse, sometimes accompanied by physical abuse, is common in high-conflict marriages. Myrna, an only child, was fourteen at the time of the split-up. She describes how she lived in fear of her father's uncontrolled outbursts and violence, and told us a familiar story of the cycle of abuse:

My dad could be good at times, you know, after he'd terrorized us and ripped the house up and beat my mom. It wouldn't last more than a day or two. He'd come back to us like there was nothing going on. Then he'd go back and then he'd feel guilty or whatever—it didn't seem right to me. But he would try to be nice.

Nora, thirteen at the time of the separation, spoke about the roller-coaster ups and downs she witnessed.

They had a relationship much like my father, my father's temperament—it was either really good, and they got along really well, because they both love to laugh, or it was the worst possible situation you could ever imagine yourself in, and it would change at the drop of the pin. A word could be said, any comment could be made, and it was all done, and my father would turn, and there would be screaming, yelling, and violence.

She went on to tell us about the anxiety she felt whenever her father was at home. She said she could just "feel" the violence coming.

I could see it in his eyes and I'd try to think of something funny so he'd forget whatever it was that set him off. I remember taking my little sister and hiding her, I was so scared that he would turn on her.

Even though serious ongoing conflicts are highly distressing to children, other factors will also play their part in determining the long-term effects of your high-conflict marriage on your kids: your children's age at the time of the divorce, their individual relationship with each parent, and a complex interaction of protective and risk factors, which will be discussed more extensively in chapter 8.

While we can't necessarily predict how a divorce will affect kids simply by knowing which of these three types of marriage their parents had, the categories can help us understand the role your marriage might have played in any postdivorce adjustment problems. If you had a good-enough marriage, you have given your children a good foundation, and can add to that by having a good divorce. If you had a devitalized or high-conflict marriage, you can take heart that the decision to divorce may have been the very best thing you could have done for your children.

No matter what category your marriage may fall into, however, you can still manage your divorce in ways that mitigate the risks to your children. Even though the marriage leaves its mark, you can help your children overcome its negative consequences by improving their emotional lives after the divorce.

CONCLUSION

In this chapter we looked at how children's home environment prior to the divorce is part of the larger picture that makes up the total impact of the divorce on their lives. We turn now to look at many other factors after divorce that combine to affect children's well-being. As these adult children look back at their feelings about their family life after divorce, they provide important lessons about what works and what doesn't. In the next chapter we will look at what adult children of divorce have to say about their parents' relationships, not only right after the divorce but also in the twenty years that followed. It is in their reflections, their twenty-twenty hindsight, that we'll understand how to minimize negative effects and maximize the possibility of a good divorce—for the whole family.

Part Two

Changes, Changes:
What Our Kids Want Us to
Know About What Works
and What Doesn't

Chapter 4

LIVING ARRANGEMENTS

What Kids Have to Say About Their "Best Interests"

E ven though more than one million parents divorce every year, most parents feel they have stepped into uncharted territory as they try to meet the needs of their family. Second only to agonizing over the actual decision to divorce, deciding where the children will live and how they will have time with both parents is the most difficult and painful decision parents have to make. It directly confronts the harsh reality that divorce will change everyone's daily lives.

One given is that *all* living arrangements fall short of the ideal. Another is that parents often disagree. They may agree that they want to have living arrangements that permit them to continue to share parenting, but how they accomplish this across two households without clear-cut guidelines is no simple task. Even in the best of situations, the decisions that parents need to make about custody and living arrangements are ambiguous, complex and often painful.

To the stresses of the daily practicalities such as child care, housing and financial concerns, add the strong emotions they each have about ending their marriage. Then layer this with their concerns about the children's welfare and the importance of their relationships with their children. It's a rare parent who doesn't feel overwhelmed. Although it certainly can't resolve all the issues of this difficult decision, listening to the views of the grown children will provide some guidelines for determining optimal living situations.

THE ADULT CHILDREN SPEAK ABOUT LIVING ARRANGEMENTS

The most startling feature of these interviews is the consistent, striking difference between what mattered to these kids and what mattered to their parents. Parents agonize, argue, negotiate and litigate over the minutia of how much time their children will spend with each of them. Mediators, lawyers, judges and mental health professionals listen to parents daily as they haggle over differences that may amount to one or two hours a week. Parents sit with complicated calendars as they calculate to the minute exactly how they will get the exact half or one-third time with their children that the plan calls for, or whether children have to be returned to the other parent before or after dinner, or whether holiday time is divided equally.

But when we spoke with this large group of adult children, they quickly skimmed over the specific time allotments and focused on issues that cut across all of the variations. Especially as they get older, children want flexibility in their living arrangements, which is difficult for most parents with their own busy work schedules. They want to have their needs considered more by their parents and be able to transition between households on their schedules, not their parents'. Feeling tied to a rigid time clock feels intrusive and unfair.

As a group, for example, they were far less concerned about the specific number of days per week or month they spent living with one parent or the other than they were about how their parents' relationship infused the emotional climate surrounding their *transitions* between parental households. As one woman noted: "Although sometimes the going back and forth was a hassle, what really upset me was how my parents kept fighting about whether I spent more time with one of them than the other. It made me feel like it wasn't really the time with me that mattered, it was only whether one of them won the tug-of-war."

Most of all, what children want is to have relationships with both of their parents. They want to feel safe and secure so they can get on with their own lives. At whatever developmental stage, children want to know that their parents will care for and love them while they continue their daily lives with as few interruptions and stresses as possible.

IN PARENTS' INTERESTS

The reality is that parents are often not able to comply with what their children want. Parents would like to meet their children's needs as much as possible, but their own needs, desires and the demands of daily living often make it difficult or even impossible.

Financial Considerations. In divorce, parents are faced with having to divide their financial assets and liabilities. How they do this and what they each have afterward will usually affect living arrangements. Many questions immediately surface. Will parents have to sell the family residence? How far apart from each other will they live? When both parents are employed outside the home, as is true for over three-quarters of American families, how will child-care arrangements be financed?

Employment Status. Are both parents employed? Is one parent the major breadwinner? How flexible are each of the parents' working hours? Do their jobs involve overnight absences? With most parents working full- or part-time today, juggling child care with busy schedules becomes even more complex when parents maintain separate residences.

Child-Care Responsibilities. To complicate matters further, as more women share the breadwinning role in the family, more men are sharing child care responsibilities. Once fathers are more involved in child care, they are less willing to be relegated to a "visiting" role when a divorce severs their marital relationship. Although this is certainly a benefit to children, it may have the down side that children have to go back and forth between homes on parents' schedules, not their own.

More Than One Child. As any parent knows, when you add several children to the mix, figuring out workable living arrangements quickly escalates the amount of complexity. Children will have different needs, depending on such considerations as their ages, their temperaments and their separate relationships with each parent. But the reality is that the majority of parents don't have the time or resources to have different arrangements for each of their children and, except in a small minority of cases, children within families usually abide by the same living arrangements, with minor alterations in schedule as specific needs arise. If we continue with the notion of making decisions based on the best interests of the child, and if the children's needs differ, on which child's needs should we base the decision?

While most parents stay locked into negotiations about living arrangements as an expression of their own power struggles, they also fear losing their relationships with their children. As they face separate lives in separate households, they are concerned about what having less time with their children will mean. Many parents are too angry at the time of the divorce to even consider the possibilities that living arrangements might change as children's and parents' needs change. This is not to underrate the importance of spending time with one's children, but only to point out that the extreme concern parents often feel may be more about *their* interests than it is about their children's.

WHEN CUSTODY BECOMES
A POWER STRUGGLE

The overriding factor in the living arrangement equation is the relationship between the parents. Practicalities of schedules become intertwined with feelings of sadness and anger and fears about loss. Married parents have the freedom to decide how involved they want to be in their children's daily lives, but as divorce looms, worry creeps in about whether and how they will be able to continue their involvement.

We must also remember that, although assigning fault is no longer a necessary *legal* component of divorce, this does not settle the *emotional* need to find fault. As you think about and tell your personal account of why your marriage is ending, there is often a need to locate a cause, and that cause is often labeled as "your spouse's fault." Once fault is assigned, of course, the perpetrator needs to be punished. In a marriage, if a spouse is angry, there are usually many small ways to punish the other, such as withdrawing or withholding affection, sex or money. But once the divorce decision has been made, the major avenues of inflicting punishment are the children and money. When divorcing couples are in the grip of issues of power and control over these two most important resources, working out living arrangements often becomes more about winning than best interests.

Fortunately, many parents are able to avoid these kinds of power struggles. But for those who can't, there are mediators, counselors, therapists, lawyers, court-affiliated professionals and judges who can help clarify when personal power struggles are preventing the making of good decisions. And it is important to remember that, although living and child-care arrangements need to be decided at the time new households are established, they can be renegotiated as lives change and personal angers subside.

Clearly, deciding children's living arrangements is extraordinarily complex. It is almost always an interplay between emotional factors, practical factors and legal issues that has its roots in societal views about gender, parenting and divorce.

Updating the Outdated Language

First, let's take a brief look at the concept of *custody*, which is the term for who will be legally responsible for the children, financially, emotionally and physically. Custody often has little to do with how living arrangements actually get worked out. In fact, most of the adult children in our study didn't even know what their family's legal custody arrangement was. It was only in those families where parents continued to battle over custody that children were aware of the precise ruling.

Many courts and professionals today are seeking to replace the language of custody and visitation with language more appropriate to the times: In place of the word "custody," they are using terms such as "allocation of child-rearing responsibilities," "living arrangements" and "parenting plans." When allocating parental responsibilities, the courts will now use such terms as "in-home parent" and "residential parent" (as opposed to custodial and noncustodial parent), terms that can be applied to either parent during the time when children are in their care. Acknowledging that legal joint custody is more a concept of parental "rights" than it is a designation of responsibilities, parenting plans are now incorporated as part of the final divorce decree. These plans spell out the specifics of living arrangements and parental responsibilities.

Because custody legislation differs from state to state, this new language and approach is not consistently applied. But this new direction reduces the ambiguity and helps parents think through and work out the nitty-gritty specifics of how they continue to responsibly parent their children across households.

How Parents Make Custody Decisions

Ideally, custody decisions are thought to be based on "the best interests of the child." However, although much has been written on the subject, there are no hard-and-fast rules about how to define "best interests." In custody disputes, such criteria as the child's relationship with each parent and which parent is to be the primary caretaker are agreed upon by most professionals, but the realities of what is in the best interests of *your* child are not easily derived from any standardized list.

Who decides what is in a child's best interests? Ideally, of course, his or her parents. But divorcing parents are likely to have different opinions. You may feel that it's best for your children to live with you because you have been the primary parent, the parent who did most of the child care. Or you may feel that your child should live with you because you are the better disciplinarian or can afford to keep and maintain the family home. Maybe one of you questions the other's parenting abilities or feels that you have a closer relationship with the child.

Here's a typical route to deciding custody. If you are in conflict over the decision, you decide to seek the advice of a professional. But you soon find out that even experts may differ about which custody arrangement is best for your child. One expert believes that one stable home is most important; another believes that spending equal time with both parents is most important. If you still can't resolve the custody conflicts, even after you've consulted the experts, by default you decide to let the court decide. If you go this route you and all your children will then be required to have psychological evaluations and perhaps you will each hire your own psychologists to testify on your behalf. Then you sadly discover that how the custody decision will be made rests not on some agreed-upon policies but by the judge who hears your case. So you listen to your friends, your lawyers, your therapists or your mediators tell you how the judge is *likely* to decide and you realize that you are caught in a confusing maze that doesn't seem to make any rational sense at all.

Why the Confusion?

Why all this confusion? Because custody determinations have been based more on our societal values than on the specific needs of individual children. If you had divorced before the mid-1800s, the decision would have been clear-cut. Back then children were treated as property and, since fathers had rights to their property, they were always awarded custody.

For the next century, emphasis on fathers' custodial rights was replaced by mothers'. As domestic life became women's domain, the "tender years doctrine" became the standard for determining custody. Quite simply, it was assumed that young children in their "tender years" needed to be in their mothers' care and therefore the presumption of the courts was that mothers should have custody. Up until the 1970s, over 90 percent of custody awards automatically went to mothers. If a father wanted custody, he had to prove that his exwife was grossly incompetent, mentally deficient, abusive, alcoholic, or drug dependent. And although it was originally meant to apply only to children under the ages of six or seven, the "tender years" standard was typically extended to older children up to about the age of twelve. If disputing parents brought their custody issues to the courts for a child over twelve, it was commonly thought that the child's desires could be factored into the court's decision.

When the gender issues of the late 1970s heated up, the issue of equal parenting rights coincided with a surge in divorce rates and divorce reform legislation. Although many divorced parents were already informally sharing child-rearing responsibilities, there was no legislation that legalized these living arrangements. Responding to these societal changes, there emerged a grassroots movement calling for such legislation. Increasingly, fathers and their lawyers challenged the assumption of mothers' long-standing rights to custody. After all, it was argued, if married parents had equal rights to their children, why should those rights terminate after divorce?

The first joint custody legislation was enacted in 1979. By 1991, more than forty states had shared-parenting statutes in which joint custody was either an option or preference, and most other states had recognized the concept of joint custody in case law. Today, every state and most European countries have some form of joint custody legislation. Now, in most of the states, joint custody has become a priority or a presumption. This means that it is presumed that since joint custody existed (albeit de facto) in the marriage, it will continue after divorce, unless one parent presents a clear case for sole custody, with well-substantiated reasons.

The underlying assumption here is that joint custody is the means of preserving a child's right to both parents and that when both parents seek to continue their roles as parents the court should not favor one parent over the other. It is intended to ensure that a child lives with both parents on some shared basis and that each parent assumes some of the day-to-day parental responsibilities. Assuming as it does that children can "live" with both parents, it is also intended to remove from fathers the stereotypic label of "visitor" in his child's life.

Although in theory states agree about joint legal custody, considerable variation still exists about its definition. Because of the ambiguity and in order to spell out living arrangements, joint *legal* custody decisions are accompanied by a separate designation of *physical* custody. Although it is not a hard-and-fast rule, joint physical custody is usually assumed to mean that between 25 percent and 50 percent of a child's time is spent with one parent and the remainder with the other. Joint *legal* custody has become the accepted norm but joint *physical* custody has not. The most common arrangement is joint legal custody with sole or primary physical custody to one of the parents, most often the mother.

Current estimates of the number of divorced parents who share parenting equally varies from 15 to 22 percent. And, as we have seen, states differ. In a few states, nearly half of living arrangements are designated as equally shared. In other states, mothers are the primary custodians.

The Ambiguities of Joint Custody

As you can see, custody decisions have been governed largely by the prevailing gender roles of the day. But unlike the earlier years when custody assignment by gender was clear, today the rules governing custody are murky.

Without a clear presumption based on the gender of the parent, the "best interests of the child" has become the prevailing legal test for custody decisions. And yet there are many complex factors involved as well as wide variations in how this concept is interpreted. Although less than 10 percent of custody decisions and living arrangements are eventually litigated in court, most others are resolved in "the shadow of the law." Matrimonial lawyers and mediators hired by disputing parents to help them negotiate and resolve their differences are guided by what they assume would happen were the case to be decided by the courts.

While not having clear-cut guidelines about child custody

may be uncomfortable, this should not be interpreted to mean it is necessarily bad for children and families. When we begin with the premise that, in general, parents have equal rights to their children and are equally responsible for them, we can then make relevant decisions about what works best for *each individual family*, factoring in individual differences of children's needs and temperaments. A good change, indeed, though certainly not an easy one.

Ambiguity always creates anxiety, but stepping backward surely is not the best way to deal with it. Joint custody is a radical change in our thinking about divorce and families, one that departs from a century-old norm that divorce meant mothers got custody of their children and fathers became visitors. New ideas take a long time to become accepted and it's unrealistic to think that in such a short time joint custody will be wrinkle-free. Rather than get rid of it because it's difficult and makes us feel uneasy, I suggest that what we need is to continue to experiment with it and make it elastic enough to meet the needs of modern families.

The Children's Living Arrangements

To complicate matters further, children's actual living arrangements are not always in concordance with the legal custody determination. For example, in the legal joint custody families I studied, less than half of the parents shared living arrangements. The others resembled traditional sole custody arrangements in which the children resided primarily with one parent and visited the other. There were also some other families in which the parents did not legally have joint custody but the living arrangements were shared.

In the rest of the families the majority of the children had their primary residence with their mothers, at least during the first few years after the divorce. Almost half saw their fathers once or twice during the week and on at least one or two weekends every month. Others saw their fathers less frequently, once or twice a month, with some seeing them as little as once every few months. Only a few saw their fathers less often. For the small group of children who had their primary residence with their fathers, almost all saw their mothers quite frequently, usually several times a week, often spending overnights. For the children in split custody arrangements, complex arrangements were usually accommodated so that siblings spent some time together in one or the other parent's household.

I expected to find some patterns, some schedules that worked better than others, but instead I found that what was okay for one child was often quite difficult for another. Over and over again, they talked about how their family's dynamics actually had far more to do with whether they were happy with their living arrangements. Unlike their parents, however, who felt such concern over time allotment, their concerns were primarily with the practicalities, their feelings about transitioning between parental homes and their desires to see more of their fathers. Before we move ahead to the children's feelings about their living situations, let's back up a moment to reflect again on the joint custody families.

SURPRISING FINDINGS ABOUT JOINT CUSTODY ARRANGEMENTS

The twenty-six joint custody families in this study were pioneers. The children of these families are the first and only joint custody children to be studied twenty years after their parents' divorces. As I analyzed the children's interviews, my own assumptions about relationships between these parents were challenged. I fully expected that simply because these children were living substantial amounts of time with each parent, we could assume that their parents were fairly amicable and cooperative. Much to my surprise this was often not the case. In over half of these families, parents were in conflict at the time of the divorce and remained conflictual over the years, both by the children's and the parents' accounts of the relationship.

Why, then, did these parents choose joint custody? In order to make some sense of why *conflictual* parents would make this choice I turned to the interviews of these parents in the first five years after their divorces. More surprises. In the majority of these families, it was the mothers who had initiated the divorce, sometimes because they found their education or careers were incompatible with the marriage, sometimes because they became involved with someone else, and sometimes because of alcoholic or abusive husbands. Many of these mothers said they "gave in" to the wishes of their husbands and compromised on the arrangements. They preferred sole custody but either out of guilt or to avoid litigation they settled on sharing living arrangements.

Many of the fathers in these families remained in the family home while the mothers moved to smaller and less expensive living quarters. Although in those years it was usually customary for mothers to be awarded the family home along with the children, these mothers were less able to afford the costs of keeping the home than were the exes, especially since sharing custody often results in the reduction or elimination of child-support awards to mothers. In only a couple of these families did mothers have a serious psychological problem, such as debilitating depression, that would have limited their parenting abilities.

It was 1979 and these parents were on the cusp of the revolution in changing gender roles and more egalitarian ideas about parenting. They were still living in the era when mothers were the primary caretakers of the children. Since maternal custody was the norm, the expectation of the courts and of parents themselves, mothers were automatically awarded custody of minor children, unless they were proven unfit. So, it is not surprising that many of these mothers felt "entitled" to sole custody, and agreeing to joint custody was perceived to be "giving up" their rights to their children. Although it is now almost twenty-five years later, and gender roles have changed dramatically, I still find that many mothers assume that they should be the primary parent after divorce. This is especially true among couples when gender roles during the marriage have been more traditional than egalitarian.

In contrast to the conflictual parents, the *cooperative* parents who shared parenting represented a different model. They valued equal parenting rights and responsibilities and believed that it was in the best interests of their children. Most of these fathers had been more involved with their children than the average father of that time and wanted to continue their involvement. The mothers respected this, and shared parenting was a welcomed solution. In contrast to the conflictual couples, these mothers did not feel like they were compromising, and most were pleased not to have to carry the full responsibility for child care.

When parents were in conflict the children were usually dissatisfied with the arrangements and, in fact, the arrangements changed, often within a couple of years of the legal divorce. Sometimes it was a parent who was dissatisfied, other times it was the child. In cases where the children were dissatisfied, some moved in with one parent for six months or a year, then often moved in with the other parent for some period of time. In a few cases the children moved in permanently with their mothers and over the years rarely saw their fathers. Some of these arrangements ended up back in court in a legal custody fight but most were changed informally by the parents or by the children.

Although joint custody is much more common today than it was twenty years ago, I think the findings from this small group of families reflect current realities fairly accurately. First, joint *legal* custody families typically have diverse living arrangements. Some have equally shared time but many do not. Second, we cannot assume that parents are amicable and cooperative just because they have joint *physical* custody and share equal time with their children. Some are, but many others are not. Joint custody, as a reflection of the gender revolution, speaks more clearly to the issue of parental *rights* after divorce than it does to parental *relationships*.

TRANSITIONING BETWEEN PARENTS

Whatever the actual living arrangements, the great majority of children with divorced parents experience coming and going from one parent's household to the other's. They have to learn how to manage not only the physical but also the psychological aspects of these crossings. As we touched on briefly in the beginning of the chapter, it was not so much the actual time they spent with each parent that mattered most. They were more concerned with how transitioning between their parents affected them emotionally and whether it interfered with their activities and friendships. Children who were over six or seven years old at the time of the separation clearly remember their early living arrangements and what it felt like to go back and forth, whereas younger children rarely remember the specifics or their feelings about it. Although a few children in the study said they just accepted the arrangements, saying, "It was just the way it was," most had strong feelings about the arrangements.

In their reflections about their living arrangements, the children make some points very clear. *Going between homes is not easy for children, but parents can reduce the stress by taking whatever measures they need to in order to at least minimally cooperate.*

The Emotional Pulls

Needless to say, the thing that stresses children most, sometimes for many years, is lingering conflict between their parents. Several children talked about how parents bad-mouthing each other put them in the middle. Travis, fourteen and the middle child of three, lived with his mother weekdays and spent several weekends a month with his father.

> It's the old thing—they were playing the kids against each other. You would hear a story from one and then get another story from the other, and you would never know for sure who is closer to the truth than the other. Now, as an adult I have learned to take everything with a grain of salt, and see where it is planted here and there.

His younger sister also felt caught in the cross fire:

> It made me really mad. I would have to try to keep my mouth shut to not upset the other. I had to really watch what I said when I was with either one of them, because— for example, if I would mention my father while I was with my mother, that would really set her off.

Unfortunately this resulted in her distancing herself from both parents. "I don't remember ever having this feeling like, oh, I can't wait to see my dad or mom now. I really miss them! Instead, it was always a relief to get away from the other."

Twenty years later, although their parents have become more cooperative and occasionally even spend a holiday together, the children *still* feel caught in the middle. Holly, now thirty-six, the oldest of the three children, says: "I was always the peacemaker. Even today, on the few occasions that we're all together, I worry about what's going to set either of them off. When

Mom starts to bad-mouth Dad I quickly jump in and change the subject."

Other children also talked about how the anger between their parents made the transitioning between homes difficult. They would often get quizzed about the other parent's life, household, or relationships, and that made them extremely uncomfortable. Tina spoke for many when she said:

> Because the divorce was just not a friendly divorce, it was hard going and coming back because there was a lot of animosity between my parents. They would question us a lot about the other parent. They put us in the position of taking sides.

Lori was nine when her parents divorced and she remembers the tension she felt when she went to her father's.

> My dad always wanted to know about my mother. He would ask question after question about whether she was dating, did any men stay overnight, did she buy any new furniture. The list was endless. I always felt like I had to protect my mother even though I wasn't sure what my father would do with the information.

Robert, who was eleven at the time of the separation, felt overwhelmed by being caught in the cross fire of his parents' anger: "We were just Ping-Pong balls. I don't think they intended for us to be emotionally disturbed about it. I don't think they intended to hurt us. It's like they were getting back at each other, and we were the information carriers."

Like Robert's parents, many parents tried not to expose their divorce resentments to their children. Some had explicit rules, like not discussing issues between them when one or the other came to transport the children, but most of the children were able to feel the hostility and were often tense because of it. As we've seen, children tend to be finely attuned to the subtleties of their parents' relationship. Take the following common situation, for example. Mom's irritation increases as the transition time nears. Dad becomes overly concerned about making sure all their belongings are picked up, ready to be returned to the other home. There's that little reminder from Mom or Dad that maybe it's better not to talk about something that happened during the visit. The result is that children often feel that they are walking on eggshells, wanting to keep the peace between their parents.

It was not all bad, however. Some children noted the things their parents did that made a positive difference. This may seem perfectly obvious, but many children made particular note of how their parents eased the transitions. "Actually they were really good about not putting us in the middle and it really made it easier. I know some divorced parents slam the other parent and stuff like that, but even though I knew there was conflict between my mom and dad, they never brought it up in front of us."

Overall, they sent a very clear message: The more cooperative the parents, the less likely that the children experienced distress as they transitioned between homes.

Children especially appreciate it when parents spend some time with one another during the pickups and drop-offs. This puts less pressure on them to be the ones in charge and they are then able to be more relaxed. Heidi, age ten at the time of the separation, remembers that her parents developed a little ritual to help make it easier for all of them. The whole family would have dessert together at her mother's when her dad came to pick them up. Ryan, age eight, remembers that he felt "taken care of" when his parents together reviewed the list of things he was taking with him to the other house. And Tony, age nine, remembers how his mother encouraged him to take his father to his room and show him all of the schoolwork he had done that week. For all of these children, these seemingly small behaviors by their parents at transition times helped children cope with the crossings.

Rituals are healthy ways to mark transitions in families. In divorce it helps children feel that their parents are connected and they are able to retain a sense of family. It normalizes the transitions between households. By extension, when each parent develops small rituals to mark their children's entry and departure from their home, it eases these transitions as well. Children often need time to switch gears from household to household and it helps when parents recognize this and make special efforts to help children settle in.

Of course over twenty years things have changed. It is not unusual today for parents to pick up and deliver children without encountering one another at all. Day-care centers, schools and after-school activity groups are accustomed to having one parent drop off a child in the morning and the other parent do the pickup at the end of the day. Some children much prefer this. The good-byes to one parent are less abrupt and they have the whole school day to shift gears. Other children, especially the younger ones, find this stressful because they can't always remember who is going to pick them up at the end of the day.

If you are not there when children are making the changeover it's important that you prepare them well before they leave you. Young children need to be reminded that it's that "special" day and older children often need help remembering what they want to bring along with them. Until it becomes a consistent part of their schedules, some children are anxious that their parents will get mixed up and they will not be picked up at all. To make sure that teachers and child-care workers are very clear about the plans, you might want to send a reminder note along with your child each time, including emergency phone numbers where both parents can be reached in case of any snafu. A child's age and temperament are important to consider when transitions are not overseen by both parents.

How Parents Can Ease the Transitions

Differences in rules and routines, the hassles of transferring clothing and belongings, and coping with travel topped children's list of dissatisfactions with the mechanics of living in a binuclear family. Although some of these dissatisfactions are part and parcel of transitioning between households, parents who are aware of the common issues that distress their children can greatly reduce many of the stresses.

Try to have consistent rules across households. Parents who divorce often have differences in their values about parenting, and living separately allows them to express these differences more than they did when they shared the same home. Some children, like Patrick, recognize this and adapt.

> There were difficulties but they were just sort of things that were normal. I think my sister and I would act differently around my dad than we would my mom just because they were different people and wanted to raise us in different ways. For instance, my mom wouldn't care if my sister and I would swear when we were at home; she didn't think that was that big a deal, but my dad thought it was the wrong thing to do, so we would have to adapt to each of their homes, and their rules.

Even though their parents may have different styles of parenting, most children want them to have similar rules in both their homes. They want their parents to consult with each other, agree on plans and not involve them in conflicts. Of course most divorced parents would like to do this but many find that their anger gets in the way.

More cooperative parents are often able to agree on some basic rules, such as bedtimes, TV watching, eating habits, and curfews.

Not only does this make it less confusing but it also cuts down on the children's ability to manipulate the situation to their advantage. Of course, all children are quick to pick up on the differences between their parents' rules, but when parents live separately and don't check it out with each other, children have an open playing field. This is not liberating but makes them feel insecure.

When parents are still mired in conflict they are not able to discuss these issues, and rules in the two households will invariably be different. Some children will prefer one parent's rules to the other's and welcome the differences. Others will play one parent off against the other. The important thing is to be aware that inconsistent rules will have negative consequences and your kids may have a hard time adjusting as they go back and forth. "It was always hard to come back home and have to make my bed, clean up my room, go to bed the same time every night," said Nathan, who was nine when his parents separated. "My mom was big on rules and Dad couldn't care less. I didn't tell my mom about what I did at Dad's because I was afraid it would start another fight between them."

In binuclear families, the "Mom always lets me do it" refrain gets played often. If parents are angry, they may respond with something like, "I don't care what your mom says, you're here now and these are my rules." Although this may work at the moment to keep your kid in line, it only serves to increase your child's feelings about the conflict between his or her parents. It is far better to say something like, "For now, let's do it my way and I'll talk with your mother and see if we can agree on what's best for you."

Make sure you're not clinging to "abide by my rules" as a power play. Instead, decide which rules you believe are *really* important to *your child,* such as getting eight hours of sleep on a school night, not having sugar before bedtime, and so on. Ask your ex to do the same. Then, if there are major differences, seek a mediator to help you find a suitable compromise.

Deciding on some common rules can be especially important during your child's adolescent years. Even married parents who can turn to each other for support find it hard to establish and reinforce rules during these years, especially when their child pulls out every argument in their arsenal to convince them that it's fine if they stay out until 3 A.M. because all the other kids are doing it.

In binuclear families, these issues become magnified, and if parents are unable to communicate, it is much too easy for their teenage children to pursue activities and behaviors that neither parent approves of. For example, at this age children are often left in charge of making their own arrangements about which parent they're staying with when. If parents don't check it out with each other, neither may know where their teenager is sleeping that night. Should this be the case it's time to find a good family therapist to help you set and enforce some mutually agreed upon limits and boundaries.

Anticipate some upset. When possible, give your children an opportunity to talk about problems they may be having with the other parent or parent's household. Let them problem solve with you. If that's out of the question, then at least understand the difference between your households and anticipate that there will be spillover from stressful times spent with the other parent.

James, who was ten at the time of his parents' divorce, lived with his father and spent time with his mother most weekends.

> The strongest memories I have are of leaving my father's house to go visit my mom. I remember that I typically felt that I had to rein in my emotions around my dad. He never was very comfortable with sadness or anger or over-happiness. We kind of maintained an even keel there. I know that when I went to my mom's, upon getting there I would oftentimes end up getting into a fight with my

mother and then crying—kind of like letting it all out. And then my mom and I were fine. There was definitely that pattern.

Parents often complain about the difficulties they have when their children first arrive and when they prepare to leave. That children feel upset during these times is quite normal. Not only are they dealing with the losses that are part of every transition but they are also dealing with preparing themselves for the changes they may need to make in their own behavior. For example, if your child is angry about having to leave you, he or she may be nasty to you or withdraw from you for several hours or longer before the transition. It is not unusual for anger at one parent to be displaced on the other. As James did, some children let out the feelings they suppressed at one parent's home when they enter the safety zone of the other parent's. It's important to be aware of what your children may feel as they prepare to cross from one parent's care to the other's and allow for a period of adjustment. Just acknowledging to your child how difficult it may be can help him settle down easier.

Make their travels less stressful. Children much prefer their parents to live close enough to each other so that having time with each parent doesn't involve having to get on trains, buses and planes. It's not just that they don't like to travel, it's more that they want to maintain the regular schedule of their daily lives. They also want to see their parents at more frequent intervals and maintain flexibility in doing so. When parents live at a distance from one another, children usually have to make most of the accommodations. Clearly this is one of those decisions that parents make in order to meet their own desires, and it's important to know that it often conflicts with their children's.

When children are young, traveling alone for many miles either by plane or by bus can be scary. Said David, an only child of six when his parents split, "It's a lot to ask of a kid. I used to have a card pinned to my jacket, saying where I was going and giving phone numbers. Someone from the airlines was supposed to stay with me, but I remember one time when no one came and I had to change flights."

Other children enjoy the experience and like getting to spend time in another part of the country. "I loved the adventure of going to see my dad," said Barbara, then eleven. "We lived in the city and Dad lived in the country and I got to ride horses and play outside all the time. As I look back on it, I remember feeling very grown-up, being able to travel on a plane by myself." Like Barbara, many children became accustomed to living part-time in another geographical area. Some make new friends, enjoy the opportunities to be with their parents' new spouses and extended family and enjoy the different qualities of each home.

If, as a parent, you have travel anxieties, it's important that you are careful not to let these color your children's feelings about traveling to see their other parent. Try to safeguard their trip by preparing them well and making sure that they bring whatever they need to make them feel more secure and comfortable. You can listen to their dissatisfactions and help them cope with the reality, remembering that once they're there they are likely to have a good time.

Parents who live far apart need to be aware of their children's ambivalent feelings. They want to see their other parent but they don't want to disrupt their lives or leave their friends. Especially in the teenage years, missing a special party or leaving a special friend for a few weeks or longer is difficult. Even though it's sometimes hard to be flexible, a parent's accommodations to a child's schedule can have positive effects on their relationship.

Understand that your children may feel torn. Several children talked about feeling disloyal about having to leave a parent. If they felt their father or mother was lonely, for instance, they often felt responsible for his or her care. A few even worried about this parent when they were with the other. As Richard, who was eight when his parents separated, looked back he reflected on his worries about his mother's loneliness when he was gone. "I was always sad when I left my mom. I used to think that she would just sit home alone and be sad until I came back." As a parent himself, he now realizes that his mother probably enjoyed having some time to herself but wasn't comfortable letting him know that.

What a parent says and what behavior they show to their children at transition time can have a major effect on how they cope. Brandon's binuclear family came to see me because Brandon at age nine no longer wanted to spend overnights with his dad. After meeting with the whole family and noting that Brandon seemed to have a good relationship with his father, I spent some time with Brandon alone. After we spent some time talking I said that I was confused about why he didn't want to sleep over at his dad's when he seemed to have such a good time with him. With a trembling lip and tears streaming down his face, Brandon told me that he was sure his mother would die while he was away. I asked him how he knew that, and he quickly replied, "Because she always hugs me when I get ready to leave, and tells me that she'll miss me and doesn't know how she'll live without me."

Although Brandon's story is an extreme case, children sometimes feel disloyal to one parent if they have a good time with the other. A parent has to be careful to not let their feelings of jealousy or anger become their children's problem. It is not a child's responsibility to make a parent feel better by giving up her own needs in order to take care of that parent. When it's time for your child to go to his other parent it's your responsibility as a parent to help him do so no matter what feelings you may have about it. If you can't do that, sometimes it helps to have a friend or relative with you at the time or soon afterward with whom you can share your feelings. If you know you will feel lonely when your child leaves, make plans to do something for yourself to help you cope with these feelings. And if you have a child who worries about you, you might tell them that although you'll miss them you have some things you are looking forward to doing while they're gone. When they return describe one or two fun things you did.

Be especially sensitive if your child is having trouble with the other parent. Although most children want to spend time with both parents and learn to cope with the differences in their parents' personalities and child-rearing values, some resent being required to spend time at one parent's home, either because they don't have a great relationship with that parent or because they don't like a new stepparent or having to share time and space with the stepparent's children.

If your child returns full of complaints about the other parent, it's important that you not fall into the trap of joining in on the bad-mouthing. It's easy to do if you and your ex aren't getting along but it's destructive to your child's relationship with the other parent, and perhaps to his relationship with you as well. When parents are living together they can act as buffers for each other. When Mom's in a bad mood and Jamie is angry with her, Dad can often defuse the situation by explaining that people have bad moods and they will pass. In binuclear families, if you are angry with your ex and your child is complaining about him or her, it is tempting to talk about it as a personality flaw rather than a temporary bad mood. Resist the temptation and instead try to be helpful by listening but not joining in.

I'm not suggesting that you overlook serious problems, however. Some of the children in the study talked about alcoholic or abusive parents, about being left alone for long periods of time, not having sufficient food or proper sleeping accommodations.

Some of these children became their parents' caretakers, unable to get their own childhood needs met because they were busy being parents to their own parents. These children were caught between a rock and a hard place.

Greg's father had custody and he spent several weekends a month with his mother. "It was scary at my mother's house. I never knew what to expect. She was a drinker and I could tell just by the look in her eyes if she had been drinking or not. A couple of times she passed out on the couch. I didn't want to tell my dad because then he would take her back to court and I wouldn't get to see her."

Erin, who lived primarily with her mother, relates how painful it was to see her dad, who was depressed and lonely. "I hated spending the weekend with him but I knew he really needed me. I used to clean up his place before I left, to try to make him feel better, but I always worried about him."

In these situations, it is important that you pay attention to your child's needs and protect them if necessary. These are difficult situations to assess accurately, but if you think it is destructive for your child, then it's important that you take action. The best way to do that is to seek professional help. Your child will need help balancing her loyalty to a needy or abusive parent and having their own needs for safety and security met.

There's simply no getting around the fact that most children with divorced parents have to transition between households and adapt to their parents' different lifestyles. That's the reality and it is not an easy task. Some children, and some of their parents, cope with this much more effectively than others. There are always some children who welcome change. These kinds of kids relish staying overnight at grandparents' houses, love to travel, and welcome sleepovers at friends. For other children, any minor change, even changing the furniture around, is upsetting. Much like the rest of the population, some people are just more adaptable to change than others.

Changes to the Living Arrangements

Perhaps one of the biggest surprises in our study was that more than half of the children changed their living arrangements at least once over the years, irrespective of the initial arrangement. These were informal rather than court-ordered changes and occurred even though legal custody usually remained the same. Their reasons for changing their living arrangements were very varied. Most of the changes occurred during adolescence. Many children who had had primary residence with their mothers changed to spend most of the time with their fathers. Sometimes, because of behavioral problems, this was at their mother's suggestion or insistence. Other times it was because of conflicts with one parent.

The most frequent reason why kids changed living arrangements was a parent's remarriage. Some didn't get along with a stepparent or their stepsiblings and moved to the home where they felt most comfortable. Some made the switch because one parent moved and they wanted to stay with the other to remain in the same school or keep their peer relationships. Some changed a few times over the years, going back and forth as their family structures or their own developmental needs changed.

Siblings who started out with the same arrangements often ended up with differing arrangements. Even though parents and children often reject the notion of having "favorites," siblings quite often expressed real differences in the way they got along with each parent. And these differences often changed over the years. Some stayed more connected to the parent they were closer with during the marriage. Others found themselves clashing with one parent during adolescence while their sibling(s) didn't. The net result was that by the time many siblings reached adolescence, they had very different living arrangements. In a number of families, in fact, the differences were extreme, with one child refusing to see one parent and the other wanting to spend the majority of her time with that same parent.

Although we like to think that siblings should like each other and feel close, in reality many do not. They may feel a bond as siblings and share common histories, but other than that, they may not have much in common. In families where everyone lives in one home, siblings don't have the option of living separately. When parents separate it can open that option, and many of the children in our study selected it. This is important to remember. Children of divorced parents can and do change living arrangements, often quite successfully.

CONCLUSIONS

Regardless of the living arrangement, children seem to get most upset when they are forced to be go-betweens. Carrying information back and forth between parents makes them feel disloyal to one parent or the other. They want their parents to pay attention to their feelings and then try to resolve the problems that are making the situations stressful.

Parents want to move on with their individual lives after divorce and often this involves changing jobs and changing residences, and children rarely like such changes.

If parents are unable to contain their conflicts on their own, then they need to seek out professionals who can help. There are many sources of help available, such as counselors and mediators. Now, in many states, there are special masters, experienced professionals who can help parents with their decisions, and parenting coordinators and consultants who are specifically trained to help divorced parents work together for the sake of their children. These professionals help parents set appropriate boundaries and mutually plan and coordinate arrangements that give priority to their children's needs. It's been more or less the norm that living arrangements remain fixed while children's developmental needs change. It is encouraging to see that many parenting plans now include planned negotiations for change. These plans note specifically that as children's developmental needs change the plans need to be reviewed and, if necessary, also changed. This is difficult for most parents but it is absolutely necessary for children. Even though joint legal custody has now become the norm, there is still much controversy over shared parenting. Although child development experts may differ, most consider that children's ages, their temperaments, their emotional ties and attachment to each parent and the ability of each parent to provide a nurturing, consistent and stable home are important factors in determining how to formulate living arrangements.

Some experts believe that children need the stability of a primary home. Although I certainly agree that stability is important to children, I don't believe it should be equated with a single home. Most important, children need the stability of maintaining meaningful relationships with their parents and extended family. They also need the stability of knowing that they will be safe and secure. Parents who keep their children's needs for stability as their primary focus can settle on living arrangements that make it possible for children to spend time with them both. As these adult children have shown us, there are no hard-and-fast rules about how much time works best. It boils down to how parents relate and communicate with each other, how competent and caring each parent is, and how each child relates to each parent. Many parents can make these decisions amicably, and when they do they usually work out well for the children. For those who can't, there are now many resources available to help them.

Today the courts and state legislatures are openly debating "What's in the best interests of the children?" Although we certainly don't have all the answers, the fact that we are asking the important questions is hopeful. If parents are in conflict, will the children benefit or be harmed from shared living arrangements? Should the courts be able to order joint physical custody when parents are in a legal battle because each wants sole custody?

What to do when parents do not live near each other geographically? And further, what to do when parents who do live near one another are sharing living arrangements and one parent decides to relocate?

The point is, there is no one-size-fits-all answer; temperament, age, relationships with each parent, sibling relationships, the relationship between parents, and parents' remarriages all combine in different permutations to create different outcomes as far as living arrangements go. But for the most part, children want to spend time with both parents, and for them the keys to making shared parenting work seem to be *flexibility* that takes their unique needs and particular parental relationships into account, *geographical proximity* so they don't have to hassle with long trips, and most of all, *good communication between parents.*

The bottom line is: *When parents can cooperate, they can make most arrangements work.*

Chapter 5

FATHERS

*The Most Vulnerable Relationship
and How Children Work It Out*

Why a chapter on children's relationships with their fathers and not a parallel one on mothers? Because relationships between fathers and their children are the ones that tend to change dramatically after divorce, whereas relationships with mothers do not. In large part this is due to the fact that, despite some movement toward dual-household living arrangements, the great majority of children still have their primary homes with their mothers. Most see their fathers a couple of weekends each month and perhaps an evening per week. Some fathers, of course, see their children more and others see them less frequently. But there's no doubt that the dramatic change of having the father out of the home shakes up the father-child relationship.

The differences between fathers and mothers and their relationships with their children don't begin with divorce. In most families, mothers spend more time with their children, are likely to be more involved in their lives, and offer more nurturance and emotional support. Fathers, still the main breadwinners in most families, simply aren't around as much and their children tend not to know them as well. When children become adults and leave home, it is their mothers who most often maintain the ongoing connection.

Of course it doesn't help divorced children and their dads that society tends to cast "absentee" fathers in a very harsh light. Book titles such as *Fatherless America*, *Throwaway Dads* and *Life Without Father* point to what has been defined as the "father problem," that is, the declining role of fathers in family life.

Poverty, delinquency, drug abuse and academic problems have all been linked to the problem of children growing up in fatherless homes. This concern about absent fathers has taken center stage in the "family values" discourse. That many fathers do not have prominent roles in their children's lives is blamed on the decline of marriage and the increase in divorce. This stance ignores the reality that many fathers are successfully fathering their children after divorce, often better than they were able to before.

The huge upsurge in out-of-wedlock births, and its increased social acceptance, as well as the rise of sperm-bank fathers (some prefer the term "donors") who are unknown to their children, and stepfathers who parent some other father's children add even more confusion to the meaning of modern fatherhood.

Then there are the stereotypes about divorced fathers. First we have the "Disneyland dad," the father who, rather than taking on the "real" responsibilities of parenting, spends his time with his children engaging only in recreational activities. A second common stereotype we hold is of the "deadbeat dad" who doesn't pay his child support. He is usually portrayed as living "the good life," squandering his money and depriving his children of basic necessities. A third is that of the "disappearing dad" who moves away, remarries, shifts his focus to his "new family," and spends less and less time with his children until he finally disappears from their lives.

As we know, stereotypes—generalized beliefs about a group that don't take individual variations into account—always have some basis in reality. Yes, some divorced fathers who see their children one or two days a month, or only during the summer or on some school vacations, fit the image of the "Disneyland dad." The question is, what *are* they to do with such limited time with their children? Is it wrong that they want their time together to be "special" and so take their kids to places like theme parks or movies or video arcades? Consider, too, that when fathers live a distance away, their children don't have friends nearby or their familiar toys or games to play with. Dads are often at a loss about how to make the time together enjoyable. Doing something fun might just be the best thing.

Yes, some fathers don't pay all or even any of the court-determined child support, but most of these "deadbeat" fathers are not exactly living the high life while their children and their mothers are living in poverty. Many are unemployed or unable to meet the increased costs of separate lives.

And yes, some fathers do disappear from their children's lives, but the reasons are not likely to be as simple as their lack of love for their children. Many of these fathers point to the continued conflict and ongoing litigation over visitation, or the repeated feelings of loss they experience associated with occasional visits. Some fathers who eventually disappear from their children's lives do so in response to the pain of being rejected by their children.

The fact is, it is difficult for fathers to participate in the everyday lives of their children when they are only with them at most a few days a month. But it's not always for lack of trying. Many fathers in our study expressed deep frustration and grief about their diminished contact with their children. They miss the daily contact that they took for granted when they were living in the same household, and finding ways to compensate for that is not always possible. When the fathers in my study were interviewed during the first five years after the divorce, most were, in fact, quite angry at not having enough time in their children's lives.

WHERE ARE THE
GOOD DIVORCED FATHERS?

We have so few models of *good* divorced fathers—fathers who are very involved in their children's lives even when they don't live with them. As is often true with new behaviors that have not yet been accepted fully, the images we do have of good fathers are most often extremes, which make it difficult for the average person to identify with them. A picture on the cover of a Sunday magazine section of a recent *Washington Post*, for example, showed a family of divorced parents and their three children, with the title "The Good Divorce: One couple's attempt to split up without tearing the children apart." The article showcased a parenting arrangement of busy divorced parents sharing responsibility for their children.

The opening scene shows Eli, the dad, doing his routine "morning thing." His exwife has to leave for work very early, so Eli arrives at his exwife's house (where the children have their primary home) before the kids leave for school. He gives them breakfast, gets them ready for school, prepares their lunches and then drops them off at their bus stop. The article continues to show that Eli and his exwife, Debbie, have an amicable and cooperative relationship and still enjoy sharing holidays together with their three kids.

Interestingly, letters to the editor mocked the arrangement. Arguably, this particular couple had a complex schedule of sharing the nitty-gritty daily work of parenting that would not be suitable for many divorced parents, but I suggest that they should be applauded for their efforts, not ridiculed. Of course the extremes of divorce, like the extremes of most life situations, are more newsworthy than the lives most divorced families live.

Let's listen to the voices of adult children as they describe their fathers' roles in their lives and reflect on how their relationships with their fathers have changed over the years. This will provide a better understanding of the key ingredients in the father-child relationship and what it takes to chart an optimal course.

WHAT ADULT CHILDREN HAVE TO SAY ABOUT THEIR FATHERS

In many families, patterns between children and their fathers—both negative and positive—are established early on and then persist into a child's adulthood. In others, the postdivorce years are marked with a stream of transitions and changes in the relationship, either because of developmental growth in the children's lives or changes in their father's lives.

Contrary to the prevailing stereotypes about disappearing or absent dads, however, *half* of the adults felt that their relationships with their fathers actually improved after the divorce. A smaller group (12 percent) felt that the divorce didn't change their relationships. Although most children's relationships with their parents generally improve as they reach adulthood, the fact that divorce did not disrupt that developmental pattern for most of these adults comes as surprising good news. The bad news, of course, is that better than one-third of the adults felt that their relationships with their fathers got worse.

When the children in our study were asked to rate on a ten-point scale whether their relationships with *each* of their parents got better, worse, or stayed the same, most reported that their relationships with their mothers remained stable over time. (Notable exceptions were those children whose mothers had serious psychological problems or remarried a man who was abusive.) When participants were asked whom they felt closest with, the great majority of them said their mothers, both before and after the divorce. Removing divorce from the picture and just looking at married parents, the majority of adult children also report closer relationships with their mothers than their fathers. It's important to keep this in mind as we look more closely at the relationships they had with their fathers.

As improved and deteriorated relationships were examined separately, and the participants talked more specifically about how and why their relationships with their fathers changed, some interesting core themes emerged. To provide further insights on other factors that impact the relationships between children and their fathers, I will integrate information I gathered from both parents during the early years after the divorce. Taken together, these different sources provide a remarkably in-depth picture.

When Things Deteriorated

That children's relationships with their fathers deteriorate after divorce is a well-known story. As we've mentioned, blame is often laid at the feet of fathers, who are painted as irresponsible and disinterested. From a father's point of view, however, many barriers make his continuing involvement difficult, sometimes impossible, such as an exwife's anger, continued conflict about child support, a maternal bias in the courts, being usurped by a stepfather, and the custodial mother moving away. In addition, when a father remarries he often finds that the demands of a new family cause conflicts that result in his seeing his children less. Here, however, let's take a look at the children's perspective on the deterioration or loss of their relationship with their fathers.

In our study, somewhat more than one-third of the children

felt that their relationships with their fathers had deteriorated. Initially almost all of them felt sad about the loss of their fathers. Some, as the years passed, felt more anger than sadness. Others wrote their fathers out of their lives. And others still longed for a relationship. The only exception was those children who felt relieved not to have to see their fathers because they were abusive, either to their mothers, themselves or both.

In fact, almost a quarter of the children who had poor relationships reported that they had witnessed abuse, and these ranged from an occasional push or shove to those who witnessed more frequent serious altercations, usually combined with excessive alcohol use. More than half of these children reported that their fathers had been abusive to them as well. Of these, the majority understandably felt relieved by seeing their fathers infrequently or not at all.

Some studies have shown that fathers are more likely to maintain their relationships with their sons. Although we did not find this to be the case across the whole sample in our study, for the small group of twenty-three children who had the worst relationships with their fathers, three-quarters were daughters. Within this small group the causes for the lack of relationship were varied, but for some it was a healthy response to a dysfunctional or abusive father.

It is important to note here that how children make sense of their father's diminished contact in their lives has a great impact on their self-esteem. If they place the blame on factors outside of their father's control, such as his need to move away because of work, they are less likely to question their role in his retreat. If they feel that it is their father's problem, perhaps some psychological impairment that makes him a bad father, they will not feel as if they were the cause either. However, if they feel that their father just didn't want to see them or that he didn't love them, they will often begin to question their self-worth or their ability to be loved.

* * *

Remarriage. The most commonly expressed reason for the deterioration of the relationship was the father's remarriage. Some children withdrew because they were hurt and angry, feeling displaced and jealous of new wives and new children. Others felt that their fathers had abruptly abandoned them in favor of a new family.

Andrea was eleven when her parents separated. She describes a close relationship with her father right after the divorce, which then declined after he remarried.

Before he got remarried there were times when I would love to go over to his house. My relationship with him changed after he got remarried and moved with my stepmother into her house. And he had to get rid of all of our toys or whatever. It changed then because of the fact that I know we thought that he cared more about her and her kids than he did about us. Maybe that's not necessarily how it was, but that's how we perceived it. Her kids got more than what we ever did.

Two years after the divorce, when Juan was sixteen, his father remarried a woman with two young children.

We started out real close after the divorce. Then he got involved with other people and as the relationships went on, my sister and I got less and less important. He would say, "You're adults now and you kids don't need me." That is hard to deal with because he is still my dad. It was like he was writing us off. He doesn't really make an effort to stay in contact with us.

Money and lifestyle changes. Some children talked about how money affected their relationships with their fathers. Over half of the children talked about economic changes after the divorce, with most feeling that their own standard of living decreased. Many moved from their family homes to apartments or smaller houses. Others had to give up extracurricular activities and/or needed to take on added responsibilities like caring for a younger sibling, because the mother had to return to work or increase her working hours. Some remember their mothers' anxiety and anger about money and constant arguments between their parents about child support. A few have memories of being told by their mothers to ask their fathers to buy them clothes, school supplies or the toys they wanted. They blamed their fathers for the financial difficulties.

Karen, the middle child of three, was ten years old when her parents divorced. She felt a major lifestyle difference between how her father lived in his remarried family and the life she lived with her mother. Her anger persisted and she saw him less frequently over the years.

> It was hard seeing the differences in his relationship with my half brother Shane and them having money and not us. What makes me really angry is that he won't talk about it. He listens but he [insists that] the way he remembers things is the way it happened. It's not the way we remembered things, so that makes it very hard to talk to him.

Gina, now thirty-one, is still angry with her father about the way he treated her when he remarried less than two years after the separation. Although she saw him weekly before he remarried, for the past five years she has had very little contact with him.

> I don't really know whether it was the divorce or just his personality. I have always resented his time with his stepkids and the money he spends on them. It was hard to see growing up, especially since we didn't have much money.

I'm still angry that he doesn't give me any money and doesn't contact me.

"Unfit" fathers. A small group of children felt uncared for by their fathers. Some blamed it on their father's personal limitations or his alcoholism while others were still struggling about the reasons for his lack of interest in them. Some noted that they had personality conflicts with their fathers, and although they continued to see him occasionally, they had only a superficial relationship. Still others felt that they never had had much of a relationship with their father and that after the divorce it just got worse. They talked about how their fathers hadn't been around much and they really didn't expect much of them.

Denise was one of those who never had much of a relationship with her father. She was eight when her parents separated, and has little memory of spending time with her father. Although she doesn't blame herself for his rejection anymore, she remembers what she felt like when she was younger.

> After the divorce I disliked him even more. I mean I love him, but I also dislike him. He made us feel like a burden. Maybe he didn't make us, but I felt like a burden. . . . He didn't have time for me. He didn't want me around, and as a child that's a terrible thing to feel.

Other children felt badly for their mothers and blamed their fathers. When children listened to their mothers denigrate their fathers, many adopted their mothers' views. These children became alienated from their fathers quite soon after the divorce. Others felt torn between their mothers' and fathers' versions of events and even as adults still felt confusion about which parent to believe.

Infidelity. Although only about 10 percent of the children were told at the time of divorce that adultery was the cause, by the time they had reached adulthood fully one-third thought it was a major cause. In a few cases it was a mother's outside liaison that broke up the marriage, but most said it was their dad's.

Sometimes an older sibling, a relative or the parent had told them about it in the intervening years. Some of these children couldn't forgive their fathers and chose not to see them.

Kim was the oldest of five children and discovered her father's extramarital relationships when she was fifteen, about a year before her parents divorced. Although she had some contact with him for a few years after the divorce, she hasn't spoken to him for the last fifteen years.

> I just totally lost everything for him. I've had no respect for him ever since. He never came back and was never able to prove . . . to me that he was worthy of any respect so I just lost all respect for him as a person, let alone a parent.

When Relationships Remained Unchanged

Two patterns showed up for those who felt that their relationships with their fathers did not change after the divorce. The majority of this group lived with their fathers for a significant amount of time, either full- or half-time. Some fathers had sole custody from the time of the divorce and others had joint or split custody. Other children changed their primary homes at some point after the divorce and moved in with their dads.

Other children who lived primarily with their mothers and saw their fathers at least two weekends a month also enjoyed their time with their fathers and in their adult lives continued to be in regular contact with them. Although these were noncustodial fathers, they remained a part of their children's lives over the years by being available to them by phone and communicating with them frequently.

When They Improved

Now we turn to those children, the 50 percent, who defied the stereotypes by having relationships that actually improved after the divorce. Although there was no single path, here are the main reasons they noted:

Because of the divorce itself. Many felt that the divorce itself was the reason why they got closer to their fathers. Some, in fact, felt that their fathers actually became more involved in parenting after divorce than they had been during the marriage.

William was seven at the time of his parents' divorce and lived primarily with his mother, seeing his father twice a week. He now lives a few miles from both his parents. His parents were "angry associates" during the early years but today they have developed a more cooperative relationship. Although William has always been closer with his mother, he feels his relationship with his dad has definitely improved because of the divorce.

It's better. I think that before [the divorce], the marriage turned him off from helping my mom, so he wasn't really into raising my sister and me when they were still married. But afterward living with my mom and visiting my dad each week helped to establish an understanding and a consistency in his involvement with us. So, I think I was able to get to know him more—and because we saw him maybe a fourth as much as we saw my mom meant that it took four times as long to really get to the same spot with him as we were with my mom, but still it is much better now.

Others, like Christina, who was a teenager at the time her parents divorced, noted that the divorce more clearly delineated their relationships with their mothers and fathers.

In a way I think it got better because I thought of him more separate from my mother. Before the divorce, it was like these are my parents, and after the divorce it's here's my mom, here's my dad. . . . I think I had more of a desire to understand what he was going through.

A few others said that as they got older they realized that they had adopted their mother's view of their father, and as they got to know him separately they realized he was not the person that their mother said he was. Others felt the divorce gave them a special opportunity to know their fathers better.

Jill, who was seven when her parents separated, lived primarily with her mother but saw her father at least twice a week. She feels her parents got along "really well" throughout the postdivorce years and that helped her relationship with her father. Several years after the divorce, her father moved farther away because of work and she then saw him only on holidays and during the summer, but they kept in close contact by talking frequently on the phone. Although she has always felt closer to her mother, she feels her relationship with her father improved after the divorce.

I think over the years it has just made us realize that our relationship requires work and energy and is not, well, on one hand is something that we can take for granted because we're always going to be father and daughter, but on the other hand you really have to make time for it and realize that it has worth and importance on its own.

A few, like Benjamin and his sister, Tanya, who were ages eight and five respectively when their parents divorced, felt their relationship got better because their father made special time for them. Their parents had joint custody and the children spent several days a week with their father. Benjamin says he's always been closer to his mother, but his relationship with his father *was* "really, really great after the divorce. We spent a lot more time together. He came to all my games and was always there when I needed him." Tanya, who feels she is equally close with both her parents, shares her brother's feelings. "He was the more nurturant parent. He is very expressive and maternal. He did a really good job. He made time for us alone even after he remarried."

Maturity. A second pattern noted by the adult kids was that maturation, not the divorce, made the relationships better—either their own or their dads' or both. A few quotes typify the feelings of this group.

It's much better. It is a bigger change than with Mom. I really didn't like him for a long time. I think he began seeing the kids as objects he had to provide for instead of just kids . . . that was heart-sickening. He realized it though and made changes for the better. He now really appreciates who I am as a person.

It's much better because I'm an adult. I don't think it changed much in the beginning because I saw him all the time and because I was young. I think the changes for the better occurred because we both got older and appreciated each other more.

I started getting closer to my dad when I started high school. And I've gotten closer to him as I've gotten older. I've found a lot of similarities between us that I didn't see when I was younger.

I think it's kind of the same thing, age. And actually I've seen my father probably more in the past five years than all throughout growing up and I think that's always nice, getting to spend time.

Increasing distance from mother. The third and final pattern was perhaps the most surprising. It turned out that for about 20 percent of the kids whose relationship with their father improved, the inverse was true for the relationship with their mother. Sometimes that worsening had to do with the child not liking a stepfather or live-in boyfriend; sometimes the stepparent was indeed violent or sexually inappropriate, often with just one of his wife's children. In a few cases the mother was psychologically impaired or had a substance-abuse problem. But in all these cases the father provided a buffer, and often an alternative living arrangement when things with the mother got too tough.

One woman who was eleven when her parents split up reports that her mother "fell apart" after the divorce. She remembers her mother being depressed, but after the divorce she began to drink more and often stayed in bed for days at a time. Her father had wanted custody at the time of the divorce but didn't feel he could fight for it. But when his daughter kept calling him and begging him to come and get her, he went back to court and got custody of both of his children. She talked about him as a "good father" who "did an exceptional job providing stability for his two children."

Some of these situations resulted in legal disputes that then resulted in changes in legal custody, while others evolved gradually and informally. In a few families, one child remained with their mother, more as a caretaker, while another sibling or two moved in with their father. Some of the children who left dysfunctional mothers felt guilty about abandoning them and the sibling that continued to live with and care for her.

Does Quantity Matter?

Children whose fathers maintained frequent and consistent contact reported that their relationships with their fathers were unaffected or improved by the divorce. A few children who spent the majority of their time with their fathers felt that their relationships with their fathers got worse. It turned out that these were children who didn't get along with their fathers but had little choice about where they lived or how often they saw them. In all of these situations, in fact, neither parent had the capacity to parent well, so the children remained with the less dysfunctional parent, the one who was willing to and could provide a roof over their head—Dad. These kids were caught between a rock and a hard place.

A common assumption is that children whose fathers have more limited contact with them after divorce are destined to lose their relationship. As some of these adult children indicate, this is not always true. Many children living in traditional custody situations experienced improved relationships with their fathers after the divorce. These children felt that their fathers were available to them, that they could phone them when they wanted to and that they were a welcome part of their dad's life. In other words, the quality of the relationship was more important than quantity of time spent together. In fact, as we have seen, for some children, having an independent relationship with their father actually improved things between them.

Some of the fathers who lived quite far away from their children also managed to have close relationships with their children. These fathers phoned or wrote consistently and made it clear to their children that they loved them and were interested and invested in their lives. Even though almost all of these fathers had remarried, the children still felt like they were very special to their dads and looked forward to spending time with them.

The answer to the question of whether the amount of time matters is both yes and no. It's important to children to be able to spend time with their fathers, and when there is more time together there is more opportunity to form close relationships. However, not having daily—or even weekly—in-person contact does not mean children cannot form a close and meaningful relationship with their fathers. What it does mean, however, is that fathers need to let their children know that they care, and by showing up at events in their lives, they let their children know that they are important. Less than frequency, what matters to children most is reliability and consistency, and a genuine interest in them.

THE EFFECT OF THE EARLY YEARS OF THE DIVORCE

Not surprisingly, the tenor of the father-child relationship is often established early on, and fathers who play the most active role in child rearing early on continue to have the best relationships with their kids over the long haul. For a noncustodial father, involvement with young children is frequently related to his relationship with his exwife. When relationships between parents are reasonably good and they are able to communicate about the children, fathers are likely to spend more time with their children and assume more responsibility (emotionally, physically and financially) and the father-child relationship benefits.

When parents continue to have conflicts even many years after a divorce, the father-child relationship almost always suffers. Children who become embroiled in their parents' disputes experience painful loyalty conflicts, and to quell the anxiety of feeling that it's not possible to love both parents, they will often side with one parent or the other. In general, because most children have closer relationships with their mothers and are more dependent on them in their early years, they are more likely to side with their mothers in disputes between the parents. Especially when they are young, they tend to believe that their mothers have good reason to be angry at their fathers, both as a way to protect their mothers and to protect themselves.

We asked the adult children whether they blamed one parent for the divorce, and if so, which. About half said they didn't blame either parent. Of those who blamed one parent, however, most blamed their fathers. The most frequent reasons given for that blame was their father's bad behavior, infidelity, absence, or his lack of ability to communicate. This blame then affected how children related to their fathers.

Children often internalize their mother's anger and align with her, which carries over into their relationship with their father. Some never become independent enough emotionally to separate out their own feelings about their father from their mother's feelings, and their relationship with their father continues to suffer. Others, as they mature, evaluate relationships with both parents and are able to make new decisions that may lead to better relationships with their father.

A second factor that affects children's long-term relationships with their father is his remarriage, especially an early remarriage. Having a father remarry within two years of the initial separation exacerbates a child's painful feelings of loss. Regardless of age, it is usually just too hard to see one's father with a new love, new life and new children so soon after divorce. As we saw in some of the examples, when children felt their father's loyalties shifted to his new family, they usually felt rejected and abandoned.

Interestingly, a mother's remarriage was far less likely to interfere with a child's relationships with either father or mother. Mothers are more likely to remarry later and, if their new husbands have children from a former marriage, these children usually reside with their custodial mothers.

As we've already noted, the children we interviewed were very attuned to a parent's infidelity, especially if it was perceived to cause the divorce. Those who weren't told at the time often figured it out for themselves later on when they realized how quickly their fathers moved in with another woman or remarried after the divorce. When this happened, the relationships were often permanently damaged. Some children grew to like their new stepmothers over time and that often helped heal their relationships with their fathers. Others who never warmed to their stepmothers or forgave their fathers grew ever more distant from their fathers over the years. We will hear more about how children feel about their parents' remarriages in the next chapter.

CONCLUSION

Children can and do continue to have good relationships with their fathers twenty years after divorce, lending strong support to the idea that although the family structure changes, families are not dissolved by divorce. In fact our finding that half of the relationships improved suggests that it is the failing or dysfunctional marriages that often damage relationships between fathers and their children and that many of these relationships can actually be saved by divorce. As we saw in chapter 3, when marriages are conflictual or disengaged, many fathers withdraw from both their wives and their children. To avoid being consumed by the conflicts between their parents, many children also withdraw. After divorce, many of these children and their fathers are able to renew their relationships and become even closer.

Moreover, children and parents don't stop needing or wanting a relationship with each other once the children reach adulthood. In fact, in some ways, these relationships may become even more important. Not only do older parents value and need their relationships with their children, but their children are the gatekeepers of the next generation—their grandchildren. As children become parents themselves, it is common for them to reflect about their childhood relationships with both parents, and many, as they mature, become more understanding and accepting of their fathers. As they look back on the emotional distance they felt with their fathers, they often yearn to reconnect.

This is especially true for children who experienced a parental divorce during their early childhood years. Both parents and children experience feelings of loss, and the father-child relationship is typically the one that suffers the most. Many discover that it's not simply "the divorce" but a combination of factors related to the changes in the family that had an important impact on their relationship with their fathers. In my clinical practice, I hear many adults question whether their father's love got submerged by the other stresses in the divorce. As children look at their parents' divorce through an adult lens, they often see a much more complex picture than they did in earlier years. Often, this motivates them to want to repair any damage done to the relationship with Dad.

To dads: In general, because most mothers continue to provide the primary care, and because children are usually closer with their mothers, fathers often have a difficult time figuring out how to have meaningful relationships with their children. Fathers need to know that when children feel that their fathers are available and caring, they develop trust and want to spend time with them. Even when children see less of their fathers than they do their mothers, the relationship can be strong if fathers go the extra step to maintain closeness with their children.

Part-time fathers who have less contact can still keep meaningful connections with their children. They can make use of today's technologies, using e-mail and online photos and faxes as well as the telephone. Many older children now have their own cell phones, allowing fathers to talk to them without having to interact at all with their exwives. The ability to videoconference on a basic desktop or laptop computer also gives fathers a chance to "visit" with their children. Although nothing beats being able to be physically present, fathers who can't be there don't have to sacrifice their relationship with their children. Children can feel strong emotional bonds to a father who they don't see often if he makes it clear that he cares for them and is responsive to their needs.

Although it is normal for parents to want to get on with their lives and form new intimate relationships, children need time to stabilize after the major changes that are a normal outcome of divorce. Putting children's needs first sometimes requires that parents postpone fulfilling some of their own personal needs. For fathers, this translates to not bringing new intimate partners into their children's lives for at least a year, or even two, after the separation. Their first priority should be to establish a good, reliable postdivorce connection with their children. When they do that, and when the children are secure in their father's commitment to them, they are more likely to be able to accept their father's new family life. The payoff to both fathers and children is a continuing relationship that will thrive and provide important benefits throughout their lives.

To moms: Mothers play a critical role in this relationship, too. In their role as gatekeepers of the children, they also need to know that they are gatekeepers of the binuclear family tribe. They can facilitate contact, or make it much, much harder. For children, the loss of a relationship with their fathers is often the most distressful and damaging part of divorce. If mothers continue to be angry, bad-mouth their exes to their children or tie visitation to the receipt of child support, they set up barriers to their children's relationships with their fathers, with long-lasting, possibly lifelong, effects. As the more vulnerable relationship, the father-child relationship is often dependent on the goodwill of the mother. You can maximize your children's resources and better meet their needs by encouraging your children to have a healthy relationship with their father.

Children usually want to see their fathers more often than they do and they want more flexibility in the arrangements. As a mother, do whatever you can do to facilitate their seeing their fathers more often and more easily. The short-term inconveniences and sacrifices to your time will have long-term pay-offs for your children. That includes looking at your part in the conflicts with your ex and doing whatever it takes to reduce or avoid them. Remember that fathers in high-conflict relationships with their exes saw their children less often than those in less conflictual relationships. They were also less likely to see their relationships improve, though some children were able to reconnect with their fathers when their parents no longer needed to interact with each other.

An added perk for both mothers and children is that when fathers maintain relationships with their children they are also far more likely to continue to contribute financial support. Not only does their continued financial support give children the message that their father still cares and is continuing to be concerned about their well-being, it can reduce hostility with the children's mother.

The majority of divorced fathers are good fathers who continue to be important in the lives of their children after divorce. Continued reliance on the outdated stereotypes of fathers is destructive to children. By increasing the visibility of good fathers, and establishing healthy models of families postdivorce, we will greatly reduce the potential risks for children.

We now move on to the next chapter to explore how the expansion of the family tribe affects children's lives.

Chapter 6

REINVENTING
THE BRADY BUNCH

How Remarriage Changes Children's Lives

U s, the Ex, the Ex's New Mate, the New Mate's Ex, and the
Kids." This subtitle of Delia Ephron's book *Funny Sauce*
describes what many are now calling the new extended family. In
wanting to extract as much humor as she can from her message,
however, Ephron adds, "It consists entirely of people who are
not related by blood, many of whom can't stand each other."
What she misses, of course, are the blood relationships between
children and their parents, the relationships that give this newly
joined tribe its very reason for being.

It is estimated that at least one-half of *all* children will have a
divorced and remarried parent before they turn eighteen. Despite
this fact, we are sorely lacking in good models of divorced and
remarried families. We only have negative stereotypes and poke
fun at the unfamiliar realities that these complex families live
with, which adds immeasurably to the stress children experience
when their parents remarry. Remarriage after divorce is so common today that three-quarters of those who divorce will eventu-

ally remarry and more than 50 percent of new marriages have a divorced bride or groom (or both).

In fact it's not unusual nowadays to attend a wedding and see the children of the bride and groom participating in the ceremony. You can even consult the grande dame of etiquette, Emily Post, to find out where the expanded cast of characters should sit or stand in the reception line. She notes, for instance, that it is acceptable for the bride to have her children escort her down the aisle, but adds a word of caution: "It is preferable to have only one or at most two of your children escort you, simply because the aisles are narrow and you don't want to look like a crowd when you are making your entrance." Some remarrying families are defying Ms. Post's suggestion and are all proudly marching down the aisle as the crowd they're about to become.

Of course remarriage is not the only path for creating new family tribes. Many divorced parents now choose to live together to avoid the legal complications of marriage. Taking that into account, the truth is that the vast majority of children who have experienced a parental divorce will expand their tribe as new family members are brought into their lives. How this next transition in children's lives affects them and whether they welcome or resent their new relatives are the topics of this chapter.

It used to be that most stepfamilies, like the Brady Bunch, were the product of remarriages after the death of a spouse; children in these families rarely had more than one living biological parent. But today, the vast majority of our stepfamilies originate after divorce, and this is where the complications begin. In addition to the many variations (twenty-six have been identified!) most children with divorced parents eventually become part of *two* stepfamilies. When the child's primary residence is with the stepfamily, it's called a "living in" arrangement. When the biological parent is the nonresidential parent, the term "living out" is used. But even these terms are insufficient. For example, with joint custody and shared parenting, children actually live in two households. Even the U.S. Census—which only started collecting statistics on stepfamilies in 1980—doesn't have an accurate count of stepfamilies. If a child spends substantial time living in two homes, which home gets counted in the census as the primary residence and which as the stepfamily unit?

Why haven't we developed new terms for postdivorce families when clearly they are badly needed? I would suggest that it's because we still cling to the notion that nuclear families are the way families are *supposed* to be. We keep hoping, in spite of all evidence to the contrary, that divorce will become a thing of the past and families will once again return to what most consider to be their original, rightful form. This entrenched belief, that "family" means one mother, one father and their children all residing in one household, makes other family forms seem deviant and deficient because they lack all their "proper" members or have additional members who don't fit the tidy family image.

WHO'S IN YOUR FAMILY?

Interestingly enough, children call whatever form they live in "family." They talk about their stepmom, or maybe that they live most of the time with their mom and Tom, her boyfriend, or their dad and his partner, Ted, or they live with their mom in Omaha and their dad lives in Chicago. But to kids, all of these arrangements mean *family*. To help children feel normal we need to give up our nuclear family bias and extend our definition to include all who consider themselves family.

Confusion results, however, when we refer to each household in the binuclear family as a *separate* family. By doing this, we fail to recognize the connection and interdependency between the two households. Changes in one household affect the other and often require new negotiations between biological parents, which are then likely to result in changes in the other household.

The experience of one of my client families provides a good example of this interdependence and how it plays out.

Sarah and Jason's parents, Bob and Sue, devised a joint custody arrangement in which the children alternated weeks between their households. When Bob remarried, he became the stepfather to two children who were close in age to Sarah and Jason. His stepchildren lived with them during the school week and spent three weekends a month with their biological dad. In order to gain one extra weekend a month free of all the children, Bob asked Sue to make some seemingly minor accommodations in Sarah and Jason's living arrangements. But Sue was in no mood to do this because she was jealous of Bob's new life and felt threatened that their children might prefer to spend more time with him and his new family. She also had a child-care situation that worked because she shared the children's nanny with another single parent whose schedule blended well with hers.

A year or so later Sue remarried a father of two teenage boys, one who lived with them full-time and spent alternate weekends with his mother and the other who lived primarily with his mother and visited on the weekends when his brother was with his father. This arrangement allowed the two boys to spend every weekend together with one parent or the other. After about six months, Sue and her new husband began to find the alternate-week schedule too unwieldy and disruptive to their routines and asked Bob if they could change the children's living arrangements. Sue wanted the children to live with her during the school week and go to their dad's three weekends a month from Friday afternoon until Monday morning. To make up for his reduced time during the school year she suggested that he increase his time with the children during the summer. Her reasoning for the change was that Jason was having trouble with transitioning every other week. Bob didn't see any evidence that Jason was having problems and he refused to make the change. The anger mounted and their conflict increased.

Bob's wife felt that he was caving in to his first wife's demands and they began fighting more. Sue's husband, on the other hand, blamed Bob's wife for preventing Bob from changing the arrangement because it would conflict with the time her children spent with them.

And what was happening to Jason and Sarah as the conflict increased? They were feeling torn between their parents, fearful of saying what they wanted because it would come off as favoring one parent over the other.

Eventually they resolved the situation by keeping the alternating schedule but changing it to two consecutive weeks in each household. The children, who by then were completing middle school, felt comfortable with this arrangement, and although neither parent got exactly what they wanted, the compromise settled the dispute and the conflict ceased.

Like Jason and Sarah's binuclear family, a parent's remarriage usually upsets the family's equilibrium. As one parent's life expands to incorporate a new partner and perhaps new children, the other parent also needs to make changes to accommodate their children's new family members. Often these changes include a renegotiation of living arrangements and other situations related to the children, like how holidays are spent or who will go to the school play. When a stepparent joins the tribe, biological parents also need to make some changes in their relationship with each other as well. These renegotiations are rarely easy. For children, a parent's remarriage often creates loyalty issues and causes earlier feelings of loss to resurface. For the other parent, it often brings up unresolved feelings about their exspouse. For the newly remarried, issues of feeling torn between two sets of loyalties are common. Most parents manage to struggle through this stressful time despite the lack of knowledge and available models to guide them. It's no wonder that some children find the time of a parent's remarriage more difficult than the divorce.

In fact, we know very little about how kinship bonds tie two-stepfamily households together. How, for example, do children relate to two female parents, a mother *and* a stepmother, or two male parents, a father *and* a stepfather? How do they deal with having multiple parents? How do they relate to their stepsiblings and halfsiblings and what happens to these relationships over the years?

I began this book with the story of the wedding of my daughters' halfsister and showed how our family ties spanned households, in spite of a lack of adequate language to describe their relationships. This deficiency in our language reflects the social expectation that these relationships (such as the one I have with Susan, my exhusband's widow) don't exist. But we know that that's not true. As we turn to the voices of the participants in this study, we will hear how children make sense of and manage their new family tribes.

WHAT DATING AND REMARRIAGE MEAN TO KIDS

Perhaps nowhere are the differences between children's needs and parents' more evident than when it comes to dating and remarriage. For parents, remarriage is a time of renewal, a chance to build a new life with a new love. While their mothers or fathers may be enjoying their courtships, however, children are worried about how their lives will change—again. Naturally, parents want their children to share in their happiness, and they are often surprised and disappointed when they don't. Children's varying reactions to their parents' remarriages depend on many factors. How long has it been since the divorce? How old are the children? Will they have to change houses? Will they have to share space with new "instant" siblings? Do they like their new stepparent? What does their other parent feel about the remarriage and how, then, does this affect their feelings?

Let's start with dating, which is a strange-enough experience for parents and their children. For parents with children at home, dating involves getting babysitters, figuring out when and what to tell the kids and when to involve them. For parents who have their children only on weekends, there is the extra challenge of not allowing your single life to encroach on your limited time with your children. For children, it turns the role of parent upside down, often leaving children feeling more vulnerable. Seeing their parents date is a reminder that changes out of their control are happening to their family.

When it comes to dating, parents are full of questions. Should they keep their dating lives separate? How serious should a relationship be before he or she stays overnight? How much attention should I pay to my child's objections? We are fortunate to have the hindsight wisdom of many children. How did *they* feel when their parents started dating? Some children were happy about it, some expressed indifference, and others felt angry, resentful or embarrassed. Almost all experienced their parents' dating or remarriage within two years after the separation and nearly one-third remember them dating less than a year afterward. Because almost a third of the children had at least one parent that had formed a new relationship (nineteen fathers and eleven mothers) before the divorce, these children never witnessed their parents' dating.

As single parents themselves note, dating makes them feel like adolescents. It brings out the same insecurities and behaviors. They become more concerned and insecure about their appearance, experience the mood shifts that go along with "falling in love" and take on other qualities that remind them of their teenage years. Children, especially adolescents, are often disdainful when they see their parents act like teenagers. As we'll see, children had different reactions to their mothers' dating versus their fathers'.

Mother's Dating

Because most children have their primary residence with their mothers, they are usually aware of her dating unless she chooses to date only when the children are with their father. A child's age is an important factor; young children, those between the ages of five and ten, tend to feel possessive of their mothers and threatened and resentful about having to share them.

> I didn't like it. I didn't like it at all—despised every one of them. Of course, I thought it was the men. It may have been that I didn't like her dating. I just thought they were skuzzy pieces of dirt. I didn't like anything about it. They were in my territory.

> I hated it. I resented him in my house—I saw it as my house. I didn't want him around, and I resented him and I fought with him, and I didn't get along with him at all. He tried to develop a relationship with me, but I made it very difficult on him.

Some of these younger children had trouble with their mother's dating because they still had hopes that their parents would reunite. This was more likely to be the case when their mother began dating shortly after the divorce.

> Well, I guess I wasn't real keen about it. I thought he was kind of weird. I don't really remember how I felt. I probably wanted my parents to get back together.

> I hated seeing my mother with another man. I remember that I was really bratty, hoping that I could get rid of him so that my father could come home again. I kept thinking

that if she couldn't find another man, that would mean they would get back together.

Other children who start off not liking the idea of their mother dating often change their view when the relationship becomes more serious. As the children themselves have time to develop a relationship with the new man in their mother's life they often begin to see benefits.

At first I was not too thrilled. But after a while Hank was around a lot and I got kinda used to him. We started to do some fun things and actually my mom did more with us 'cause we would all do stuff together.

Older children also have a range of feelings, both good and bad. Many feel uncomfortable with their mother's affectionate feelings and resent having to be around their mom and her new man.

My mom would have this man over at our house for dinner and I didn't want to have anything to do with him and I think that's why I didn't like my mom dating—because I didn't like having to be a part of it.

I really hated it when they acted like kids. Every time I left the room they would kiss. She seemed to get silly around him and I just wanted to tell her to cut it out.

I was very unhappy. I think I thought it was creepy. As a teenager I understood why she was dating and I don't think I ever expressed any discontent out loud but I remember weird feelings.

For teenagers, who are busy grappling with their own bewildering sexual feelings, dealing with their mother's overt sexuality can be confusing and troubling.

My mom was more like a rebellious teenager, she did all the stuff teenage kids feel uncomfortable or embarrassed about. She took up disco dancing, wore bikinis in the summertime and all that stuff.

I thought it was okay for her to date, but she was like a teenager. She mooned around waiting for the guy to call. She changed her clothes ten times before going out. She kept asking me how she looked. She wanted me to greet the guy at the door and actually have a conversation with him while she was still getting ready. I just wished she would meet him someplace else and keep me out of it.

Many older children are fine about their mother's dating. Especially if their parents' marriage had been very bad or if it was a long time before their mother started dating, they are pleased to share their mother's happiness and are often relieved that she is beginning to have a new life.

I encouraged her to go out, because I felt she deserved it. After everything she had gone through, she deserved to be happy with somebody.

I couldn't have been happier. After almost five years, it was time. We tried to get her to go out earlier but she was too scared to, I guess. Finally, this guy from work called her for a date and we all made her go.

Father's Dating

Children are often more upset when their fathers start dating. As we saw in the last two chapters, many already want to see their fathers more often than they do, and when their fathers begin dating, the children often feel threatened that they will become even less available.

Some children also feel upset because they are protective of their mothers. If their mother is upset or angry about her ex's dating, the children are also likely to be distressed. Many view their father's attentions to other women as a direct insult to their mothers. It is not surprising that these feelings become more intense when he is with the woman who they feel caused the divorce.

Children are often particularly distressed when fathers involve their children with their new partners. They don't want to lose their special time alone with Dad. Of course this is also often a matter of scheduling and convenience; dating usually happens on weekends, when children are more likely to spend time with their fathers.

The loss of attention was a common theme expressed by many children who reported that they felt angry, hurt and jealous because their fathers' dating took away precious time that they wanted to spend with him.

I wasn't pleased, I wanted him all to myself because I didn't see him as often as I saw my mom. I would play sick so he wouldn't go out.

He was always gone, at work or out with girlfriends. It irritated and upset me a lot.

I didn't like it 'cause he wasn't around for me. He wasn't there on the weekends, so I was angry at the people he was dating. "You're invading my space . . . he's mine."

Adolescents can already be very judgmental of their parents, and their angry feelings are exacerbated when they deem their father's choice of women inappropriate.

He was out a lot on the weekends and was inconsistent about what he told us was right and what he did. It was a big irritant for me. He'd be out late on Saturday night and then he'd make us attend church and then he would go in and fall asleep. And at home, he'd come in the next morning in the clothes he had worn before kind of thing.

I didn't like it. It was just somebody else to take time that we weren't getting. And, of course, his first girlfriend was a lot younger — she was young enough to be my sister, and we were both very embarrassed about that. My dad just holding hands with her at the mall was so embarrassing!

I was really uncomfortable, and initially I was hurt. It seemed as if he was always around younger women. I got disgusted with it because of his infidelity with younger women, with less desirable women, women he would pick up at a bar.

Children usually prefer to be less involved in their father's dating life. The reality is that most children don't really want to know very much about their parents' new single life.

He was very careful and made sure he didn't date when we were staying with him. When he had a date we were never around. I never met any of his dates when we were younger. I was really relieved by that.

I didn't mind it as much because I didn't live with him and it wasn't really something I was always aware of. He was never really openly affectionate so it wasn't as embarrassing for me. I just wasn't as aware of his dating overall, which made it easier on me.

Children who are older and who are worried about their father's living alone often feel happy and relieved when he seems to be enjoying himself again.

It was a relief. I felt better that Dad was going out and having a good time. I didn't have to worry about him as much.

Whoa, the ol' man has still got it. I was happy for him. Dad's intention was to be happy, not to find a soul mate or remarry. He just had a normal single guy's life.

The Anomalies of Dating

Only a small group was upset about *either* parent's dating because they still had hopes that their parents would get back together. This actually came as a real surprise. Most of the literature about the effects of divorce on children finds that children yearn for their parents to reunite. Although young children may feel this, it doesn't appear to be so for the majority of children. Memory, however, is a selective process and it could be that for the adult children in this study these feelings were present at an earlier time but have since diminished in importance. Another possibility, of course, is that most of the children never had these hopes or expectations in the first place and the literature is wrong.

Listening to the children's voices as they remembered their parents' dating it's quite clear that it's a strange experience for them. Children want their parents to act like parents and dating just doesn't fit with that image—not for children or their parents.

No one is quite sure how to behave. It helps when parents are prepared for their children's discomfort and don't expect them to embrace the situation. That's not to suggest that parents tolerate rude behavior from their kids. But they can let their kids know that they hear their feelings *and* expect them to have good manners and treat their friends with respect.

A FEW THINGS TO KEEP IN MIND

Remember that your children are not particularly interested in your single life and would prefer not to be a part of it.

To ease their distress *don't expect them to form a relationship with an adult who may disappear from the scene shortly.* Wait until you feel fairly certain that this new person in your life has a commitment to stay around for a while before you put your children through the difficult process of seeing you repartner.

It can be very upsetting to see parents with different partners who are there one day and not the next. Some children are likely not to know what to make of it. It can increase their distrust about the stability of relationships and they may resist any form of attachment. Your children are still feeling the effects of the family changes and seeing a new romantic partner may rekindle their feelings of sadness and grieving. It also can make them angry to feel that their other parent is being so quickly replaced.

Feelings of loss are common responses to a parent's dating. Whether it's the loss of the family as they knew it, or the loss of their fathers, or the losses felt because of the numerous changes in their lives, most children need time to get over their anxiety and sadness. When parents begin dating before children have time to cope with the changes brought about by divorce, it compounds the effects of their earlier losses. For fathers, this plays out as a threat to the already limited time most children have with them. For mothers, it was the loss of their special attention, that special single-parent time that had come about because of the divorce. While children may be distressed by a parent's dating, remarriage requires more complex changes and presents a new situation with many unknowns.

THE GAINS AND LOSSES
OF REMARRIAGE

While children may have problems coping with their parents' dating, the big adjustments come when a parent moves in with or marries a new partner. As stepparents and new siblings enter their lives, children usually experience both gains and losses. Often they feel the loss of their special time with a parent, but when they develop good relationships with their stepparents they have more adults in their lives to nurture and guide them. Age and temperament always play a part in determining children's reactions, but we also have to look at other factors such as the timing of the remarriage, the other parent's feelings about an ex's new spouse, the child's feelings about the stepparent, the economic circumstances, and the living arrangements. As you can see, the complexities are far too numerous to allow for any simple answers about what remarriage means in children's lives.

What we can predict, however, is that most children will experience a parent's remarriage fairly soon after the divorce. The children in the study saw 70 percent of their fathers and almost 50 percent of their mothers remarry within five years of the divorce. By twenty years postdivorce, 87 percent of their fathers and 72 percent of their mothers had remarried at least once. In fact, in only four of the eighty-nine families were both parents still single twenty years down the line.

But that's only a piece of the complex picture of how their families changed over the years. In two-thirds of the families children gained *both* stepmothers and stepfathers—and usually stepsiblings, too. In fact, in only a few of these families were no new siblings added. Remarriages and additional siblings weren't the only changes, however. About a quarter of both the remarried mothers and fathers had a second divorce, and some of these parents are now in their third marriages.

The Stresses

Children, especially when they are young, don't draw a distinction between cohabitation and remarriage. The only thing that's relevant is that a parent's new mate now lives with them and is a consistent part of their daily lives; the legal marriage contract is irrelevant. There are no formal terms to describe children's kinship with a parent's unmarried partner and his or her children, but when these relationships become reliable and stable over time, children think of them as step-relationships. For this reason, I will not make a distinction but will consider both cohabiting and married partners as stepparents.

Even though a parental divorce is difficult for the great majority of children, almost a third of the children we interviewed said that the remarriage of a parent was even more stressful. In addition to adjusting to a new adult parent figure, remarriage often results in a change in relationships with one or both of their biological parents. When the primary custodial parent remarries, it can also involve a change in homes and schools and a loss of friends. In many situations it results in the children living farther away from their other biological parent and seeing him or her less frequently.

When Dad remarries, the biggest threat to the children is that they now have to share their already limited and precious time with him with another person and possibly other children. This was the case for many children in our study who found their fathers' remarriage more difficult than their mothers'.

Relationships with Stepparents

The label "stepparent" certainly doesn't evoke images of someone we think of with great affection. In fact, it is hard to find any
positive images of stepparents in the culture. This negative societal view has implications for both stepparents and their
stepchildren. Neither one knows how they should treat each
other, what they should expect and what's normal to feel. Many
enter the situation expecting the worst. Given all this uncer-
tainty and negativity, it is surprising that the majority of children
in our study have good relationships with one or both of their
stepparents. Two-thirds feel they have a close relationship with
their stepfathers while somewhat less than half feel close to their
stepmothers.

Of course stepparents don't function in isolation. Their relationships with their stepchildren are related to other relationships
in the binuclear family. For example, how a biological mother
feels about her exhusband's new wife can influence her child's
feelings about the woman as well. If a child hears her biological
parent bad-mouth his ex's new spouse, the child is likely to
accept her parent's negative feelings as proof that the stepparent is
really a bad person. The fact is, children view their stepparents in
a variety of ways, many of them quite positive, if not quite of the
status of a parent. We found five general patterns for how children viewed their stepfathers and six for stepmothers.

Stepfathers

The age of the child, the personality match between a stepchild
and stepparent, the relationship with each biological parent and
the amount of time spent with a stepfather influence the role he
takes in their lives. Since most mothers are still the primary residential parent, most stepfathers live with their stepchildren.

While some children who are close with their stepfathers have poor relationships with their biological fathers, others who have poor stepfather relationships are close with their biological fathers. Still others are able to maintain good relationships with both while a small group of children have poor relationships with both. The children described their relationships with their stepfathers in five general ways:

Like a Dad

Close relationships don't happen instantly. They take many years to develop and, like any parent-child relationship, there are good and bad times. When children are young at the time of their mother's remarriage they are more likely to think of their mother's new husband as a father, especially when he lives with them a majority of the time.

At first, I just thought of him as married to mom, but then he tried to fulfill more of a father role, and he actually did. I always wanted to build bridges, and he was the driving force for that. He was a math teacher, and he showed me how important math was in building bridges. He was a very, very strong influence on me.

It didn't happen right away but we grew really close over the years. My kids love him, they call him Grandpa.

Substitute Dad

Some children, especially those who have poor or nonexistent relationships with their biological fathers, find in their stepfathers the fathers that they wished they'd had. These children usually were not close with their fathers even before the divorce and the divorce only made them more distant.

He has been very kind to me. I don't know what having a real father was like because my biological father was just out there. It is safe to say I love him. He is like a substitute father.

We get along great. He's more like a dad than my own father. We both worked on it because we both wanted it to be good.

My stepdad is an incredible man. He's raised me and I'm an extension of him. He taught me how to be a man, you know, how to define myself. . . . All the things a father's supposed to do he did for me.

Bonus Dad

There are others who are fortunate to have close relationships with both their father and their stepfather. They enjoy the benefits of having two dads. This is most likely to occur when the biological parents have a fairly cooperative relationship and the children are not caught in distressing loyalty conflicts.

I love him just like my dad. I consider him and my dad as the same.

It's not typical of the father-daughter thing I have with my dad. I can joke around with him. If I need help on my car or something I can call him and he will help me. We get along really good. He seems more like a kid kind of dad, because he likes more kids stuff.

Sometimes, however, loving two dads does cause some children to experience loyalty conflicts. In the words of one of the women,

I think it gave me some sense of feeling like a family. He gave me a little bit of knowledge of what it would be like to have a dad, because he would do things with me, because we would go to the mall, and the park, and I could talk to him about not wanting to wear dresses all week long—or whatever my mom wanted me to do. He did a couple of fun things with us, that a dad would do, that my dad never did. But, I always had my loyalty to my dad, which made it hard. He told me that he never wanted me to call another man Dad, so I could never bring myself to call him Dad—to this day. My brother calls him Dad, but not me.

Friend, Pal, Mentor

And finally, some children don't form child-parent relationships with their stepdads but they still enjoy good relationships with them. They describe them more as friends or important mentors than dads.

I don't think of him like a father but I like him and I trust him. I go to him when I have problems. He's a good listener and I know he really care about me.

He's a really good friend. It's different than a dad, but it's hard to say how. I just don't see him as my dad, but we've gotten closer over the past few years.

Having a relationship with him has benefited me more than I can describe. He's been my mentor, he helped me go to college, and now he's someone I go to when I need advice. I have enormous respect for him but I don't think of him as my dad.

"Wicked" Stepfather

The mean or abusive stepfather is not nearly as pervasive as he is portrayed to be, but unfortunately there are some stepfathers who resent or take advantage of their stepchildren. Some children in the study reported having alcoholic stepfathers who were angry and abusive, not only to them but to their mothers as well. In other situations, there was no physical abuse, but strong personality conflicts made living with them intolerable. Some of the children in these situations left their mother's homes and moved in with their biological fathers while a few remained at home so they could protect their mothers. Most of these remarriages dissolved in divorce within five years.

Stepmothers

As we turn our attention to the children's relationships with their stepmothers, let's first consider the complexities of these relationships that make them different from those with stepfathers. Relatively few children live full-time with their stepmothers because their primary residence is usually with their mothers. In fact, of the roughly 13 million women who are stepmothers, only 8 percent live with their stepchildren full-time. The rest have stepchildren who come and go from their lives, some spending up to a half week, many spending at most a couple of weekends a month or less.

Since many fathers remarry before their exwives do, stepmothers tend to join a child's life earlier than stepfathers do. Mothers frequently feel betrayed and angry when their exhusbands marry shortly after the divorce. Children may experience their own feelings of abandonment and are likely to be protective of and loyal to their mothers. In this case, stepmothers end up being seen as the enemy, the person responsible for the loss of their fathers.

In addition, men tend to marry second wives who, on average, are four years younger than their first wives. This means that a child's stepmother is often younger than her mother, sometimes considerably so. Adolescent children especially find it difficult to relate to a youthful stepmother as a parent figure. Boys of this age may feel sexually attracted to their stepmothers while girls can feel as if their stepmother is a sexual competitor.

We tend to idealize mothers in this culture—viewing them as all-giving and virtuous, the basic and often sole providers of love and nurturance—and that makes us prone to viewing stepmothers in a critical light. The mothering role is central in most women's lives so it is no surprise then that some biological mothers feel possessive and threatened by another mother stepping into her territory. When this is the case, one way children can protect their mother is by refusing to like or accept their stepmother.

Most women still assume major responsibility for child and home care and mothers and stepmothers often have competitive feelings and hold strong expectations about what women in the family are *supposed* to do. I remember one binuclear family I was seeing in counseling in which a mother was angry at her children's stepmother because the children's clothes weren't washed when they came back after a weekend with their dad. It would never have occurred to the mother to be angry with her exhusband, because she considered it his wife's responsibility to see that the children were sent home with clean clothes.

As we saw in the last chapter, relationships between children and their fathers after divorce are more vulnerable to deterioration. Stepmothers, as an extension of the children's father, are subject to the same vulnerabilities.

Given these complexities and the negative stereotypes that still prevail in children's fairy tales and in our culture in general (the "wicked stepmother" is still very much with us), it is surprising that almost half of the children in the study have good relationships with their stepmothers. The other half range from polite to tolerant to outright hostile. Six general themes capture their feelings.

Almost Like a Mom

Although some children think of their stepmothers as second moms or "momlike," it is common for them to quickly add that she isn't their mom. Their loyalty to their mother is likely to make this distinction an important one for them.

> We have a very good relationship. From the start she treated me like she does her own kids. I think of her as almost like a mom, but not quite.

> We weren't that close at the beginning, because I didn't take an interest in her. I never had a problem with her as long as she didn't try and parent me. I think I made that abundantly clear to her—that I had a mother, so there wasn't any void for her to fill. I've never had any resentment toward her. We have a wonderful relationship now. She's a great lady. I really like her. We get along great.

> I respected her as an adult, but of course there's always a part of you that's aware that this isn't your mom. In many ways she was very unlike my mother. By mutual consent we just rode the middle ground between parent and nonparent.

A Good Friend

Although some children have trouble putting a name to their relationship, they clearly feel like it is close and meaningful. For many in this group, these feelings didn't happen immediately but developed slowly over the years.

It's hard to know how to describe our relationship. I guess I think of her as a friend. I would describe her as a very close friend. But, then, yeah, I mean I've probably known her like twenty years.

She is one of my best friends. I think of her more as a friend than as a parental figure. I am close to her. She's an important part of my life and is involved in everything. I can talk with her about things I don't feel comfortable talking with my parents about.

I'm very lucky. She was great from the start. She would take me to do something new every time. It wasn't always something big or expensive, but it was just always a really enriching experience. I always felt special to her.

Mediator

Some stepmothers play an important role in their stepchildren's relationship with their father. In some situations, relationships with their fathers actually improve because of stepmothers.

Sometimes I'm able to talk with her more easily than I can to my father. He's a very strict and by-the-book type of person who just wants the best for his daughter. Sometimes when things arise in my life Sharon will be more understanding about it, so I can vent through her and it will pass to my father with a spoon full of sugar.

We get along good, we joke around quite a bit. I think she's excellent for my dad because he seems to have gotten his act together, she reined him in, in a good way. I actually like my dad better since he's been married to Maria.

We have a really warm and friendly relationship. She really cares about me and my family, and what's going on. She's an important connection between me and my dad. My dad is the type who believes no news is good news, so he doesn't call often, but Shelley calls just to see how I'm doing. He travels a lot and she also lets me know when he's in town. She's definitely helped my relationship with my dad.

Civil and Polite

Some relationships resemble many extended family relationships. They're not overly close, they're not great, but they're not awful either.

We have what I would call a formal relationship. We have surface conversations and can chitchat but there's nothing more than that. I was already a teenager when they married and I just never spent that much time with her.

I would say it's someplace between okay and good. She's just a stepmom. It's not a real strong relationship, but there's nothing bad about it.

We're very different people. I have nothing against her but I have nothing in common with her either. She's often not around when I'm with my dad, and that's okay with me. But when she's there it's fine too.

Interloper

There are also stepmothers who are viewed by their stepchildren as getting in the way of their relationship with their fathers. Many feel jealous of her and instead of the relationship improving over the years, they continue to feel that she has a negative impact on their lives.

From the start, our relationship was nonexistent because I refused to see her for the first few years after she and my dad remarried. I felt like she had taken my dad away and I didn't want anything to do with her. Now we're polite most of the time but I really don't like her and I never have.

I don't hate her, but there's a lot of things about her I don't like. I think she's changed my dad a lot. He can't be himself around her and us. When he came to visit the last time, he came by himself. He was joking and funny, whereas if he would have brought her, he wouldn't have been like that.

After she came into the picture I never got to be with my dad alone anymore. It's like she was always jealous or something. She would plant herself in the middle of everything and it just changed our relationship.

"Wicked" Stepmother

For some children, personality conflicts with their stepmother prevent them from ever having a good relationship. Some of these children tolerate their stepmother only because she is married to their dad and others avoid her as often as they can.

She was just a mean person. We didn't get along. For example, we would get home from school, and five minutes later she would be yelling at us, going off on us. There wasn't an easing-in period, I guess. It was like all of a sudden she was there and telling us what to do, and it was like,

I thought, "Who the hell are you?" She was only a few years older than my older brother and there she was, wanting to be my mother.

I do not get along with her. I do not care for her except for the fact that she is the mother of my brother, but other than that I would not be disappointed if my dad divorced her. I just look at putting up with her as a necessary evil, if I want to see my dad.

My brother and sister and I have never liked his second wife. If my father wasn't married to her, I wouldn't associate with her. She would not be my friend, and if she was my neighbor, I'd probably move.

Are Stepparents "Real" Moms and Dads?

Although most parents know that their children love them, both mothers and fathers often feel jealous when their children form close attachments to a stepparent. I would suggest that this jealousy is steeped in our beliefs and social customs that there can be only one mother and one father in a family. As children show us all the time, they are, in fact, capable of forming loving relationships with stepparents that in no way diminish the love they feel for their parents.

Let's not forget that feeling close to a stepparent and giving him or her the status of parent are not synonymous. Again, there are gender differences. For those children who feel their relationships with their stepparents are close, two-thirds consider their stepfathers as parents while somewhat less feel the same way about their stepmothers. The others, who feel close but don't consider their stepparents to be parents, describe their stepparents as friends or mentors.

What do most stepchildren call their stepparents? The large majority address them by their first names. Even those who consider their stepparents as parents are more likely to call them by their first names rather than Mom or Dad. How, then, do they introduce their stepparents to their friends? Most say "my stepmother" or "my stepfather" or they use their stepparent's first name. Older children will often say "my dad's wife" or "my mom's husband" while younger children often introduce them as Mom or Dad.

It is important to note that while there were some differences in their feelings toward their step*mothers* versus their step*fathers*, these differences are not related to the child's gender. Boys and girls both viewed their stepparents in similar ways.

Even though relationships with stepparents have many variations, children have some common pointers for parents and stepparents.

To Parents

Give children time to get to know their future stepparent. Among the study participants, most of the children knew their mother's new partner well before the remarriage because their mother had cohabited with her future second husband and the remarriage had been anticipated. When it finally took place, it didn't represent a major change in their daily lives. On the other hand, a significant number of these children were not even informed about their father's plans to remarry. Some barely knew his new bride. In a number of situations, fathers didn't tell their children until after their remarriage and, in several situations, children found out about the marriage after the fact through extended family.

Heather was nine when she heard the news about her father's remarriage.

We found out that they had gotten married by a fluke from my aunt. For some reason my mom had talked to her, I don't exactly know why, and that's how she found out and then she told us. It was six weeks after they were married and I was really pissed.

For Scott, who was eight at the time, not being informed damaged his relationship with his father.

I was devastated. I met her only a couple of times and I had no idea they were planning to get married. Then, out of the blue, one weekend when I was over there he said that they had gotten married the weekend before. I couldn't believe he didn't tell us. I can't forgive him for that.

Sometimes fathers don't tell their children about their upcoming marriages because they don't want their exwives to know. They are concerned about arousing or increasing her anger and many are worried that it will be used as an opportunity to request an increase in child support. Though the father's desire may be to avoid conflict, the children end up feeling left out or abandoned and are likely to trust their father less. It sets the stage for children to dislike their new stepmother. But when children got to know their stepmother prior to the remarriage they also felt more accepting of her and the planned marriage.

Don't expect your children to jump with joy. Unless children have formed a good relationship with their future stepparent prior to the remarriage, they are not likely to be happy about their parent's remarriage. When they also have to accept stepsiblings their anger and resentment will probably increase. Being told that they have to share their bedrooms now with new siblings makes this situation more difficult.

For some children, as we will see, these initial negative reactions changed and they grew to like, and even love, their stepparents and stepsiblings. For some others their negative feelings about their parents' remarriage marked more problems in the years ahead.

Make some special time to spend alone with your children. Sometimes parents, in their eagerness to solidify their new remarriage family, want to spend all their time together in the new family unit. Although it's an understandable desire, children need to feel like they still have their separate and independent relationship with their biological parent. Spending time alone with your children and doing a special activity just with them alone during the time they're with you is very helpful. Your children will be less jealous of your new family when you make sure to let them know that the special bond between you still matters.

Make sure your children continue to have some special place in your home. Children often have to give up some of their space to accommodate a new stepparent and stepsiblings. Even if the room that they once had to themselves now has to be shared, it's important to make sure that whatever they leave in your house is still theirs and theirs alone. It's good to have a special place where they can leave their things knowing that they will be there when they come back. Children feel protective about their belongings, and given all the losses and changes they're experiencing, it is very important for them to feel they still have a place in your home that is special.

Don't demand that your biological children accept your stepchildren as their siblings. Allow your children, at their own pace, to form their relationships with each other. Sometimes children enjoy having new playmates but they may not be willing to accept them as siblings. Give them time to develop a history and expect some jealousies to surface.

To Stepparents

Stepparents are not instant parents. Young children view most adults in their lives as parentlike and that makes it easier for a stepparent to quickly move into a parenting relationship. It's another story, however, if the child is a teenager. Few teenagers accept a parent's new partner as a parent. It's normal for them to challenge your authority at every opportunity. The harder you try to act like their parent, the more likely they are to resist. Take the time to develop a history and form a friendship. And, as we have seen, you may never become a parent but you have a better chance to become a friend if you allow the relationship to proceed slowly.

Let your partner take the major responsibility. Fewer changes in parenting roles will result in less resistance to you. It's important that rules about behavior not be changed too abruptly and that when changes do need to happen that the biological parent take the lead. Stepparents should take a supportive role in parenting but should not try to be the primary parent.

Don't be possessive of your spouse. Sometimes stepparents feel jealous of the time and attention their spouse gives to his or her biological children. Discuss these concerns privately with your spouse but don't act on them in the children's presence. It's important to respect the special time that your partner spends with the children and for you not to compete for his or her attention when the children are present.

WHEN NEW SIBLINGS JOIN THE TRIBE

Most children gain some new siblings when their parents remarry. Some immediately gain both maternal and paternal stepsiblings, sometimes followed shortly with new children born to the remarriage—half siblings. When divorced parents marry, they usually hold out hope that all their children will learn to love and respect one another, eventually "blending" or merging as one family. This merging of children with their step and halfsiblings is further complicated because the children usually don't live together under one roof on a daily basis. As we saw in the case study at the beginning of the chapter, Sarah and Jason acquired "instant" siblings, maternal and paternal stepsiblings, the children of both of their stepparents. The three pairs of siblings came and went between their biological parents' homes on different schedules and Jason and Sarah lived with each of their stepsiblings for some period of time during any given month. If either of their parents then had a child with their remarriage partner, Sarah and Jason would have acquired yet another sibling, a half brother or sister, who would also live with them only some of the time.

How these relationships with step and halfsiblings develop over time is a subject we know almost nothing about. In fact, we know little about sibling relationships in general. What we do know is that they come in all shapes and colors. Stepsiblings can be older, younger, the same age, same or different genders, have the same or different ethnic or religious backgrounds and live varying amounts of time together. Erma Bombeck summed it up well in a column she wrote twenty years ago:

> We racked up stepchildren three years younger than their stepmothers, brothers who couldn't begin to spell their sister's last name, and grandmothers who were never too sure who you were. . . . If there's one area that needs a storage unit for names and relationships that can be printed out in a matter of seconds, it's the stepfamily.

Although we tend to attribute certain characteristics to full sibling relationships, certain expectations of closeness, love and loyalty (which are often more myth than reality), we don't have a set of similar norms for step and halfsiblings. However, in addition to the shared biology of halfsiblings, there are some other characteristics that are important to keep in mind when looking at the possible differences between these two types of sibling relationships.

Whereas stepsiblings become instant siblings, with no shared history, when children gain a halfsibling, they know this child from the time he or she was born. By the time the child is born, they have usually had time to adapt to the remarriage of their parent and can anticipate the new halfsibling's arrival. Needless to say, the half sibling is always younger. Although these differences don't necessarily determine the quality of the relationships among siblings they do help us understand some of the differences in the way step- and halfsiblings bond.

In the Binuclear Family Study, almost three-quarters of the children had stepsiblings. Of these, about one-third lived with their stepsiblings for at least some period of time. The other two-thirds saw their stepsiblings only when they all spent time at the same household or at extended family celebrations. For some, this amounted to only a few times a year. They also gained half siblings. One-third of their parents, twice as many fathers as mothers, had new children in their second marriages. Although most of the children lived for some period of time with these half siblings, a small group never did.

In one-fifth of the binuclear families, children had *both* step and halfsiblings. These are the most complex families, especially for the few who had all the permutations of maternal and paternal half and stepsiblings. We'll begin first by looking at the stepsibling relationships.

Are Stepsiblings "Real" Brothers and Sisters?

Less than one-third of the children in the study think of their stepsiblings as brothers or sisters. Those who do are more likely to have lived with them, either for partial weeks or for an extended period of time. Remember that in chapter four I noted that about half of the children changed their living arrangements and moved back and forth between parental homes. These changes sometimes created situations wherein the children lived for a year or more with their stepsiblings.

But if they don't think of stepsiblings as siblings, how do they think of them? Their responses ran the gamut from cousins, acquaintances, friends, to distant relatives, strangers and enemies. Age differences, frequency of contact, and personality issues all entered into the equation of defining what these stepsiblings meant in their lives. Their diverse responses were impossible to categorize but a few quotes provide a flavor of some of the relationships.

It was just more fun than anything—because we just saw them at Christmas and during the summer. They were significantly older. They were adults. By the time I was twelve they were either in college or out of college. To me they were like cool and I wanted to talk to them and be with them, but to them we were just two younger kids who were in the way. We were an annoyance to them. But I was intrigued by them.

We don't get together and do stuff, but when we do we get along fine. We would go to each other's wedding. They're not family. I mean, they're stepfamily. I don't really have a desire to talk to them every weekend.

I spent very little time with her. But I was resentful that when she came to see her father, she wouldn't have to do all the work that I had to do. She would get to stay up later, and stuff. Now, we see each other every now and then, but it's uncomfortable just because we don't see each other that often. She is not anyone I would hang out with.

I'm friends with my stepsister on my dad's side. My stepbrothers on my mom's side are perfectly nice people. I like them but I just don't know them that well. The one that I've seen the most I've probably only seen four or five nights since I've known them.

Up until a certain point I tried to have them as my brothers and sisters, but they weren't very receptive so I think at some point I just gave up. I see them every once in a while when I go home but it's kind of like they're just vague acquaintances.

As teens we got along really good. I mean at first I didn't like her, and felt jealous of her because I thought she was taking my father away, so I was really mean to her, but later we got along good. We're not close anymore because we live far apart, but on the few occasions we do see each other, we say "I love you" and I think it is definitely like sister love.

We have a very good relationship, we have our disagreements, but really nothing big. We get together and do things. We talk to each other every other week or whatever. He's getting married and I'm in his wedding. He was like my older brother, if people ask me if he's my brother, I won't think twice, he's my brother.

It's bad. They don't like our family. I think that because their father left his wife for my mother. Last time I saw them was a few years ago and we hardly spoke.

Are Half Siblings "Real" Brothers and Sisters?

The picture with half siblings is much clearer. In contrast to how they think of stepsiblings, almost all the children think of their half siblings as brothers or sisters.

Make no mistake. It's not that all the children jumped for joy when their mother or father announced that she or he was going to have a baby. Some children, especially those in their early or mid-teens, thought it was "weird." Said one woman who was thirteen when her mother announced that a new baby was on the way, "It was completely embarrassing. I didn't know how to tell my friends." In one situation, when a father announced his wife's pregnancy to his three children from his first marriage, his then fifteen-year-old son ranted and raved, "That's disgusting. You're much too old to have a child. It's not fair."

But even though some of the children remember being upset at the time, they now feel that their half sibling was something good that came from their parents' divorce. As one woman said, "It's pretty amazing, isn't it, that you can have a divorce and have good stuff come out of it?"

Others describe a big-brother or big-sister relationship.

We have a good relationship. I would describe it as a big brother–little sister relationship. I feel close to her—and feel more like her brother—her big brother in this case—than with my stepsisters.

Me and my [half] brother were very close. We fought a lot, but we fought about stupid stuff, like brothers and sisters do. Which was probably a lot of learned behavior because my mom and stepdad fought all the time. But when anything dramatic happened with my mom and stepdad we were instantly bonded.

I have an awesome relationship with my half siblings from my mom. We are as tight as real brothers and sisters, maybe even stronger. It's great with my dad's kids too, but I just don't see them as much.

They are like my real brother and sister. I don't think of them as "half." They wish they could see more of me and don't understand why I live in the city, but when I visit, they never leave my side.

I was completely thrilled. I had always wanted a brother or sister and finally I was going to get one. It's been great!

A few children, who were considerably older than their half-siblings, felt very parental toward them.

She is more like a daughter to me than a sister, because when she was little I was very responsible for her. After I moved out, I didn't really have much contact with her. But, we are close again now, and I still feel like I am the closest to her. She's my first girl.

I feel like a surrogate father to my half siblings. They are teens now and I often go over to see them and check up on them. I sometimes get into an argument with my dad and stepmom because I don't think they're being strict enough with them.

There appear to be few, if any, differences in relationships between full siblings in a family and between full siblings and half siblings. In fact, the greater typical age difference in a full/half sibling relationship may decrease the possibility of sibling rivalry and make it even easier for a close bond to form.

Don't Expect "Instant" Bonding

Sibling rivalries are just as common in binuclear families as they are in nuclear families. In both family forms, children have different relationships with each of their parents and strive to be special to their parents. Feelings of loss are common in divorce and children are likely to feel that their relationship with a parent, usually with their father, is threatened by the arrival of new children in the household. This is especially true if the remarriage quickly follows the divorce and children and parents have not had adequate time to develop their independent relationships. Parents need to realize this and not expect their children to feel like "instant" siblings.

As we saw earlier, some children develop relationships with their stepsiblings that are close and others don't. When children feel secure in knowing that their parents love and value them, and when they do not feel threatened that their stepsiblings will replace them in the hearts of their parents, they have a better chance of developing good relationships. Being aware of these needs and making sure to continue to spend time alone with them (perhaps even increasing the time early on in the remarriage) can help children more easily accept their new family members.

The most common mistake newly remarried parents make in their desire to form their new "family" is to quickly establish consistent rules and rituals that pertain to all the children. When that happens children are likely to feel threatened and angry and blame their new stepparent and siblings for the unwelcome changes to their lives. Parents can set the stage, try to minimize jealousies—and then hope for the best.

ENTER THE STEPGRANDPARENTS
AND OTHER STEPKIN

In nuclear families, extended family relationships, such as relationships between children and their grandparents, usually depend on how close their parents are with their own parents. This holds true for binuclear families as well. When a stepparent is close to his or her own parents, stepchildren are also more likely to see and spend some time with them. Whether stepgrandparents have biological children, how many grandchildren they have and what their ages are all contribute to the nature of the stepgrandparenting relationship. Some children, especially if they are young when their mother or father remarries, form close bonds with their stepgrandparents. Others feel like they are family but are more hesitant about the nature of the relationship.

Although most of the children in the study had met some of their stepparents' family, few had strong, enduring relationships with them.

They've always sent Christmas presents, there's always birthday presents, there's always Halloween cards. They're very much my grandparents. And although they're very doting and very generous with Jason [her half brother], they're not necessarily the exact same way with us, but that's because they've known Jason since he was born. They really try though to be very fair.

Since I've been on my own I've not stayed in as close touch with my stepmother's parents as I would have liked and I'm hoping to renew that relationship this next year. I think that it's been a process of me growing up and moving out into adulthood. I regret that. It's definitely changed — I was very close to them.

I never knew my stepmother's siblings, but I have always called her mother Grandma, and we used to go visit her during the summers. I always felt kind of strange, though, when I was in her house, like I shouldn't be there. But I still call her Grandma and give her hugs and kisses when I see her.

If they had a cookout at their house, a lot of times my stepmother will have her parents over, or one or two of her sisters, and then if I was over there, I would talk to them. They're very nice. Just acquaintances, nothing too much different than what I have with my stepmother.

SECOND DIVORCES: WHAT HAPPENS TO STEPRELATIONS?

As we have seen, many steprelationships are tenuous. What happens to these relationships after a divorce depends in large part upon how long the marriage lasted, how strong the relationship was between the child and his or her stepparent, and the nature of the divorce between the biological parent and the stepparent. When a second marriage is brief or tumultuous, relationships with stepparents and stepsiblings usually cease. However, when the second marriage lasts long enough for the children to develop strong relationships with the stepparent, some of them continue these relationships for years afterward. Others, however, mourn the loss of their stepparent. For a few, those losses extend to their stepsiblings and other extended family.

One-quarter of both the mothers and fathers in the study experienced a second divorce and were cohabiting or in a third marriage when the adult children were interviewed at the twenty-year postdivorce mark. For many children the second divorce and remarriage represented another difficult major transition; a few expressed relief because they didn't like their stepparent. Many of the parents' second marriages lasted less than five years and deep bonds had not formed with their stepparents or other steprelations. For a few children, however, not only did they lose a stepparent to whom they had formed a close attachment, but they lost their stepgrandparents as well.

> We had a really good relationship with my stepdad's parents until my mom and stepdad divorced. Now we don't hear from them. They were our grandparents. We called them Grandma and Grandpa.

For many children, the second divorce exacerbated the losses they felt during the first divorce. As we will see in the next chapters, for some children it was this accumulation of losses that created the most serious problems in their lives.

CONCLUSION

One thing is certain: remarriage involves family changes that are complicated and confusing. We need to have realistic expectations. It is important to allow for a shared history to develop so that binuclear family bonds can form. Whatever precarious balance has developed between exspouses as parents will need to be rebalanced to include new spouses and perhaps new children as well.

These are not tidy families. The relationships are not always close and there's no question that they *are different.* But even though they don't fit the Norman Rockwell image, to the people living in them these messy extended tribes are family. These are the folks who are going to sit around the Thanksgiving table together for years to come. These are the families who are going to be there to support each other and share in each other's celebrations and sorrows.

The single most important factor in making these tribes work and, as we shall see in the next chapter, the key to helping children make their way into adulthood with a sense of family intact, is the quality of the parental relationship after divorce. With parents who can communicate and negotiate and accommodate, children have the best opportunity to thrive.

Chapter 7

THE IMPORTANCE OF TRIBAL ELDERS

Adult Children Tell Us How Parental Cooperation Matters

When Kimberly received her law degree last spring both of her parents were there to celebrate the happy event. As Kimberly talked about the graduation, she reflected on how pleased she was that they were both in attendance.

I still have these awful memories of when I was in the fifth grade and had the lead in a school play. My parents had split up a couple of years before and they were still really angry. My dad was sitting up in the balcony and my mom was sitting downstairs and when it was over I looked for my dad and he was gone. My sister said he left right afterward because he didn't want to have to talk to my mom. Even though I was glad he was there I was hurt and angry that he had to avoid me because he wanted to avoid my mother.

It's really different now. It gave me a good feeling to see them sitting near each other, and that night Dad and my stepmom, Natalie, came to my mom's for the party. It's not that I want them to be together again, because I don't even think about that, it's just that I want to share my special time with both my parents.

Like Kimberly, most children want to share their special occasions with *both* of their parents. Again and again I hear that how parents relate to each other after divorce still very much matters to kids well into adulthood. It matters in terms of how holidays and special occasions are celebrated. It matters in terms of their relationships with their parents. And, most important, it matters in terms of whether they feel as if they still have a family.

Any conclusions about how divorce affects children into adulthood must underscore how the nature of their parents' relationship is intricately interwoven into all aspects of their lives. Thus far we have seen how it plays a major role in their living arrangements, in their long-term relationships with their fathers and then how it carries over into the new relationships that are formed when one or both parents remarry. It is this postdivorce parental relationship that forms the delicate foundation upon which the binuclear family is built.

"WE'RE STILL FAMILY"

Clearly, becoming an adult does not end a child's desire for family. It's important not to mistake this, however, as a yearning for one's parents to still be married. That's not the issue. It is clear from the results of our study that the great majority of adult children accept, and even respect, their parents' decision to divorce, but that doesn't negate their desire to continue to share important occasions, their joys, and even their sorrows, with their parents—together.

As we saw in chapter 1, the myth that exspouses must be bitter enemies contradicts the blatant reality that in a parental divorce children continue to be an everlasting bond between their parents. In addition, as we have seen, many people still cling to the destructive belief that the inevitable outcome of divorce is that children forever lose their families. While of course it is true that some children do end up suffering this loss, it is just as true that many other children continue to have two parents who, although divorced, coparent effectively, and they do so even after their children reach adulthood.

With few rules and limited positive models, parents enter unfamiliar terrain when they divorce. Clearly any decision to divorce means that spouses feel angry and hurt, but less known is that most of us also have lingering tender or loving feelings as well. It is these ambiguous feelings that are responsible for much of the turmoil in the first year. Add to this the common societal messages that it is only appropriate that we *should* make a radical break with the past after divorce, and it is not in the least bit surprising that divorcing parents have limited visions of how to continue their family bonds.

In fact, there are many variations in how former spouses *really* relate. Some have warm and friendly relationships, others are distant but cordial and still others are antagonistic. How do some parents effectively continue their parenting bond while others cannot? How does their relationship change when their children become adults? How do children feel about the relationship between their parents? As adults, how does it affect their meaning and experience of their family? The answers to these questions are the subject of this chapter.

PEERING INTO THE FUTURE

Over the years I have listened to many divorcing parents in my clinical practice talk about how much they look forward to the day when their children are grown and they won't have to have anything more to do with their exes. As they fantasize about how they will finally be freed from the stresses of shared parenting, I can't help but think of all the occasions yet to come that will still draw them together.

Carefully, I will remind the mother sitting across from me that no matter what their age, her children will still want their parents to share in their lives *as a family*. There will be the usual birthday celebrations, the college graduations, the weddings, the birth of grandchildren, and so on, that she and her soon-to-be ex may both want to attend. Then I ask the father if he can envision a grandchild's first birthday. Can he form a picture of the event that includes all of them, including, most likely, new spouses or partners? How will they relate?

As these parents peer into their futures, they learn to put aside their current disagreements as they face the prospect of forever being tied together through their children—and their children's children. They realize that the family they created will not end with the divorce and that it behooves them to find ways to continue to function well *as a family*.

It is certainly true that as children move into adulthood and parenting no longer requires day-to-day decision making, divorced parents have less and less need to be in frequent contact. No more long phone calls negotiating who will be responsible for what or whether this is my Thanksgiving or yours or why your child support payment didn't arrive this month. But, if family ties are to be maintained, there will continue to be occasions that bring both parents together. Whether these times are comfortable or stressful depends upon the type of relationship that parents—and stepparents—develop with each other after the divorce.

THE IMPORTANCE
OF THE EARLY YEARS

The first few years after a divorce are critical ones for both children and their parents. It is common for disagreements over child
support, custody and visitation to become the battlefields where
marital angers and disappointments get acted out. But it is during
these years that parents establish new rules that affect how children begin to cope with their rearranged family. As the chaos of
the first year after divorce diminishes, some parents manage to
settle the major tasks of the divorce while others remain mired in
power struggles.

Based on our three sets of interviews with parents, spaced at
two-year intervals, we found four major patterns that reveal how
time affects these exspouse relationships. Over the six years since
they divorced some of their relationships improved, some deteriorated, and others remained unchanged. Each of the patterns has
distinctly different characteristics and each affects children differently. After we look at these early patterns and how they affected
children we'll turn to the adult children's views of their parents'
relationships twenty years postdivorce and see how their parents'
relationships continue to have an important impact.

Four Defining Patterns

The most difficult task for parents in the early years after divorce
is figuring out how they will live separately and still continue to
parent. How to meet children's daily needs, how new living
arrangements will work, how to share some of the many parenting tasks, how holidays and special occasions will be shared or
divided. As parents try to disentangle their marital lives and still
maintain their parental ties they have to deal with the immediacy
of these multiple tasks. In the midst of their own distress about

the divorce, they have to establish separate lives and at the same time continue to have contact.

Counter to what we might expect, the quality of a couple's marital relationship does not always predict how they will relate during and after divorce. Although the communication style they develop during marriage does have some impact on how they deal with each other during the divorce process, many other factors come into play. Was the decision to divorce mutual or one-sided? Did it seem sudden to one partner? Was there a new lover waiting in the wings? Other factors are related to the individual personalities. How angry are one or both partners? Is one partner depressed? Does a spouse want revenge for wrongdoing?

In our study, some parents who had good-enough marriages managed to maintain some goodwill during the divorce. Others managed to control their anger during the separation. But some exploded in anger, either when the separation occurred or during the divorce negotiations. Some spouses, especially those from devitalized marriages, managed to suppress their anger during the marriage but could no longer do so once the divorce process gained steam. Most of the parents who had high-conflict marriages also had high-conflict divorces, but some of these parents actually managed to *minimize* conflict during the divorce process.

Conflict-Habituated

This term describes the couples who were as angry six years after the divorce as they were when they first separated. They remained stuck in their anger, mired in the past instead of moving on to the present. In fact, many of their marriages were also highly conflictual and the divorce didn't provide much relief for either the parents or their children. The parents often did little or no planning before one partner moved out of the house so that routines and daily patterns were disrupted suddenly, leaving children confused and anxious. Sometimes the only relief for the children was that, because their parents no longer lived under the same roof, the children witnessed fewer fights.

Child support, custody and visitation issues remained the ever-present battlefield where parents acted out their marital angers and disappointments. For many, litigation still continued, with no resolution in sight. Jeremy was nine when his parents separated, and he ended up switching homes three times by the time he was eleven because of his parents' custody battles. He spoke angrily about having to change schools, move to new neighborhoods, and abruptly leave friends and school activities. "I ended up always feeling like an outsider and stopped trying to fit in. Why bother getting involved when I would only have to move on again? I was a pretty withdrawn kid and never quite got out of it." Such rapid changes in living arrangements, schools and friends will tax the coping abilities of most children and have the potential to lead to insecurity and intimacy problems. I say potential because, as we shall see later on, some children will react to such conditions by actually becoming *more* adaptable and independent as adults.

Several children in our study remembered being very angry when they were placed in the untenable position of being asked to decide which parent they wanted to live with. Others remembered living with ongoing anxiety, not knowing what the courts would decide. Some experienced long separations from one parent or the other, as conflicts over custody and visitation remained unresolved.

Parents who are unable to resolve their conflicts are also unable to move on in their own lives. In such situations, life continues to be unstable and stress mounts, often creating situations that deplete a parent's ability to cope. Of course children need their parents to recover from the psychological distress associated with their separation; it's important to the children's own ability to adjust and cope.

In conflict-habituated couples, men were more often the initiators of the divorce and they also remarried sooner, most within two years after the divorce was finalized. As we saw in chapter 5, children's relationships with their fathers suffered more when their fathers remarried soon after the divorce. Compared to the other patterns, physical and substance abuse by one or both parents were also more prevalent in this group. The mothers, most of whom had primary custody of their children, also reported higher levels of depression and anxiety. Compared with the other mothers, fewer in this group had remarried.

These couples represent the worst-case scenarios and fit right into the cultural stereotypes. The marriage was destructive and the divorce offered no resolution. It is the children from these families who are at greatest risk of developing long-term problems. It is worth noting that while a little over 40 percent of these couples stopped relating altogether over the years, an equal number actually improved their relationships. This improvement could not heal all the damage of the past, but it did reduce stress for the adult children. (The remaining 20 percent were still acting out their conflict twenty years later.) Why were some children more deeply affected than others by the ongoing conflict between their divorced parents? Why did some of these kids of conflict-habituated parents reach adulthood with severe social problems while others felt distresses but managed to work around them? Because some children are more vulnerable and others more resilient (due to temperament or access to outside resources that help buffer the risks). We'll hear more about these children when we discuss resilience in the next chapter.

Steadfast Cooperatives

This term describes couples at the other end of the continuum. Most of their marriages were either good enough or devitalized. These couples were largely cooperative from the time they divorced and remained so six years later. They were likely to have orderly divorces that minimized the disorganization. This gave them time to negotiate the changes, which helped their children begin to cope with their anxieties about the disruptions in their family routines. Although the changes were difficult for the children, parents were, for the most part, available to meet their needs. While few of these parents considered themselves actual friends, they clearly felt that their love for their children ties them together.

Jan, ten at the time of her parents' divorce and the oldest of three children, has good memories of her parents' marriage and made a fairly easy adaptation to her parents' divorce.

> I remember being very sad when they told me they were going to divorce. I was afraid that they would start having terrible fights like my friend's parents did, and that my dad would go away. But that didn't happen. In the beginning I remember Dad coming over a couple times a week to help me with my homework, and I would spend most weekends with him. When Dad moved closer to our school we slept at his house a couple of nights a week too. I liked it better when they lived together, but it wasn't as bad as I expected. Mom and Dad both still came to my soccer games and other events.

Like Jan, children of cooperative parents tend not to experience dramatic changes in their lives after divorce and their relationships with both parents continue along, uninterrupted by the household changes. In the midst of their own distress, parents manage to remain focused on the needs of their children and they try to maintain some stability in their lives. Having developed a history of compromise and cooperation, these steadfast cooperative parents were able to maintain a process of coparenting that supported their parenting. Legal issues had been settled, the mental health of almost all of the parents in this group was well within the normal range, and most had remarried. Over half of the parents who chose joint custody fit this pattern.

Most children in these families have the double benefit of a cooperative parental relationship both during the marriage and after the divorce. Although many are certainly surprised and saddened by the divorce, their parents' ability to ease the transition with their continued cooperative coparenting buffers the impact of the divorce. Loss is an inevitable part of the divorce process, but these parents minimize the relationship losses by both maintaining frequent contact and good relationships with each other and their children.

Cooperation Enhancers

These parents started out as contentious at the time of the divorce, but six years later showed marked improvement in their relationships. Most were from devitalized marriages, although surprisingly, a few actually had high-conflict marriages.

My own divorce from my children's father fits this pattern. When my exhusband and I separated after a marriage that had become devitalized, with open conflict erupting only in the last few months, we quickly became adversarial foes. It took two years for us to legally divorce and then we were able to slowly become less acrimonious. We lived a thousand miles apart, rarely talked with each other and relied on letters to make plans for the children. It wasn't until about three years after we were legally divorced that we improved enough to progress to some minimal cooperation.

As I think back now to how things changed for the better, I realize it was a matter of time, and maturity. We seemed to stabilize about five years after we separated. We had less to fight over, we were slightly less angry and we even had a couple of positive experiences. By then living arrangements were settled and the plans for the time the children spent with their father were routine. I think he knew I wasn't trying to keep the children from him and I knew he wasn't going to try to take them away from me. We had both remarried and that resulted in a major improvement in our relationship.

Shortly thereafter we had our first "foursome" get-together—the celebration of our daughter's high school graduation. It was tense at first, but by the end of the weekend we were all more at ease. Knowing there were more occasions to come, I think we were both relieved that we could survive the festivities of the weekend together.

Over the next twenty-five years we had no major flare-ups and we remained cooperative, celebrating some family events together, occasionally having good conversations about our children, even sharing some humor now and then.

Most of the couples in the study who fit this pattern had similar experiences. There didn't seem to be one pivotal "event" that explained the improvement in their relationship. Maturity, remarriage, a new job, a child's illness, school plays and soccer games all came up in their stories. Six years after the divorce, no one in this group had plans to return to court, and patterns of living arrangements for the children had stabilized. Although the noncustodial fathers were not completely satisfied with the living arrangements and wished they had more time with their children, many noted that there was less stress and more stability in routine.

For most of these children, their parents' marriages had been good enough to meet their developmental needs. It was the early transition of the divorce process that brought on the major distress. For many, the combination of a good-enough or devitalized marriage with the correction of a de-escalation divorce was sufficient to buffer the long-term consequences. For others, the gradual improvement in their parents' relationship was not enough to counter the psychological distress of the earlier times.

Conflict Amplifiers

The couples who fit this pattern started off somewhat cooperative, expressing anger only occasionally, and became more contentious over the first few years. Most of the couples who fit this pattern had marriages that were divided across all three marital types.

A striking characteristic in this group was the obvious lifestyle disparity that developed between many of these exhusbands and wives after their divorces. Like those parents who were conflict-habituated, more fathers than mothers had remarried, many soon after the divorce (often within one year). Some mothers faced economic downturns and were jealous and angry at their exes who appeared to be living more affluent lifestyles. Child support payments continued to be an issue and the parents persisted in their use of litigation to try and resolve disputes about money and visitation. Some parents in this group reported alcohol abuse and there were higher levels of depression and anxiety.

So, how does this all add up? Parental separation ranges from, at best, a disruptive transition to, at worst, a traumatic event that has long-term consequences for families. Using the study couples as our reference point, the good news is that about 40 percent of divorced couples had cooperative relationships, either from the start or within the first few years of the divorce. The more distressing picture is that about 60 percent stayed mired in their conflicts or their anger actually increased over the first few years.

Many parents in these conflictual groups had emotional problems that likely preceded the divorce and had high-conflict marriages as well. Whether the children in these families would have been better off had their parents not split is unknown. As we will see in the next section, some of these parents were actually able to improve their relationships when their children became adults.

Some degree of conflict between divorced parents is normal, of course. And establishing how much and what kinds of conflict are most distressing to children is difficult. Certainly we know that when conflict erupts into physical abuse or gets out of control it makes children fearful and insecure. Ongoing and unresolved conflict that pervades the daily lives of children is also very destructive, especially when parents embroil the children in their arguments. Any time a child becomes triangulated like this, forced to take sides with one parent or another, it creates anxiety, stress and loyalty conflicts. But varying degrees of less overt conflict usually have less detrimental effects on children. This is especially true when parents offer each other some basic support—helping each other out in emergencies, remaining reasonably flexible and accommodating to schedule changes, taking turns taking the kids to doctors' appointments and activities, seeing each other as a resource, and so on. This tends to act as a buffer for children, mediating some of the negative effects of their parents' conflict. Simply put, being unable to resolve conflicts puts a lot of stress on parents and often impairs their ability to cope well with the ongoing challenges of parenthood. If this is the case for you, I urge you to get some professional help. Children need their parents to recover from the psychological distress associated with their separation; it's important to their own ability to adjust and cope. And as they reach adulthood, they need to know that their parents can join with them as family from time to time without the threat of conflict erupting.

THE EARLY YEARS:
THE CHILDREN'S MEMORIES

Knowing that parents and children often filter family history through different lenses, I fully expected that I would discover discrepant views. But that was not the case. In fact, the majority of children and their parents held quite similar perceptions of the postdivorce relationship between the parents. It seemed especially remarkable because, whereas the parents gave their assessments in the years immediately following the divorce, the adult children's views were retrospective; they relied on memories that were twenty years old.

What this concordance between children and their parents' views suggests is that children really do know what's going on between their parents. It was only the children who were under six or seven at the time of the divorce who didn't remember their parents' immediate postdivorce relationship, just as they didn't remember their parents' marriage. Of course we must be careful not to conclude that these young children were unaffected by their early living situations; all we know is that they had no distinct memories.

The older children didn't always know the content of their parents' arguments, but they knew when conversations went awry. Telephones slammed or furious mumbling while reading a letter did not go unnoticed. Pamela, a wise ten-year-old at the time of her parents' divorce, told us: "I always knew when my mother was upset with my dad. She didn't tell me directly, but she was snappy and I remember her crying and slamming the door to her bedroom. I was scared and angry that my father upset her so much."

John, who was seven at the time of his parents' divorce, remembers how he used to hate when his mother called while he was at his father's house.

> Everyone just got uptight. They didn't yell or anything, but my father would be impatient. He would say that he didn't see why she had to call and check up on him. They tried to be polite but I always knew they didn't like each other.

To their credit, many parents tried hard to shield the children from their acrimony. While every child picked up on tensions, those parents who were most successful at keeping theirs private caused less distress in their children.

TWENTY YEARS AFTER DIVORCE

The good news is that twenty years after divorce the majority of the adult children felt that their parents had relationships that were relatively free of conflict, and they enjoyed the benefits of sharing special times as a family. For the others, the persistence of interparental conflict caused them to feel a sense of fragmentation. Although most of those whose parents were still conflictual continued to have some relationship with each of their parents and both parents sometimes attended special celebrations, it was tense for everyone. Only a few children had no contact at all with one of their parents and, as we saw in chapter 5, it was always fathers and their children, not mothers, who had severed relationships.

When their parents were interviewed, their relationships were evaluated for the degree and type of conflict between them. Added to this we assessed whether and how much they supported each other as parents. From these interviews five typologies of divorced parenting relationships emerged. When we interviewed their adult children we gave them descriptions of each of these five categories and asked which of them best fit their parents *now*. They were also asked a number of other questions about how they thought their parents' relationship impacted their lives, both at the present time and over the years.

Before we review their responses, let's look at how the categories were presented to the adult children. As you do so, you might also try to place your parents or yourself into one of the categories.

Perfect Pals

These divorced parents are good friends. They talk with each other once or twice a week; they plan things together, and sometimes get together without the children. They may have occasional arguments but they don't result in angry disputes.

Cooperative Colleagues

These divorced parents cooperate and consult with each other about the children, but they don't have a personal relationship with each other separate from the concerns of the children. They try to share parenting of the children, are able to compromise in dividing up the holidays and may occasionally spend time together with the children (such as a holiday or birthday).

Angry Associates

These divorced parents tend to have an argument and feel angry most of the time when they have to talk to each other about plans for the children. But they talk to each other at least every couple of months, sometimes even once or twice a week, and make some joint decisions about the children.

Fiery Foes

These divorced parents rarely talk to each other and when they do they tend to be angry and argue or fight. They don't want to see each other, and avoid contact as much as possible. They are still very angry about the divorce. They are not able to work out arrangements for the children without having an argument and may need a third party (for example, lawyer, friend, child) to settle their disagreements.

Dissolved Duos

These divorced parents totally discontinue contact with each other and one parent usually disappears from the children's lives. This parent typically leaves the geographical area in which the rest of the family lives.

THE ADULT CHILDREN'S VIEW OF THEIR PARENTS' RELATIONSHIP

Most of the adult children reported that their parents got along fairly well now that they were grown. Half said their parents were now "cooperative colleagues" and another 10 percent described them as "perfect pals." Only 22 percent said their parents were still "angry associates" or "fiery foes" and 18 percent said their parents were now "dissolved duos."

Did their parents' relationships change from the time shortly after the divorce to the present, and if so, how? Many felt that their parents' relationships had improved over time. If you can remember back to the section on the four patterns of relationships between their parents in the early years after the divorce, you will recall that we found that 40 percent of the parents were cooperative while 60 percent were conflicted. Now we find that the percentages are reversed: 60 percent are cooperative and 40 percent are either conflicted or dissolved.

The most surprising findings, however, showed up in the group that described their parents as "perfect pals." The number of parents who could now be called good friends increased fourfold between the time of divorce and twenty years later. Although still a relatively small percentage of divorced parents, it is interesting that, at least according to their children, there are a sizeable group of parents that become good friends twenty years after they divorce.

Perfect Pals

Dana, now married with two children, was eight when her parents divorced. The third oldest of four children, she and her siblings all remember their parents as having a conflictual marriage and rated their parents as either angry associates or fiery foes shortly after the divorce. All agree that they are more like perfect pals today. Both parents have remarried and her mother is now divorced from her second husband. As Dana talks about her parents' relationship now, it is clear that major changes have come about.

> They just get along great now. My mom even enjoys talking to my dad. He just became a different person. I know that when my mom and he divorced, he didn't want it at all. It was my mom who wanted to, so it took him years and years to get over that, so I think now in their older ages they've come to terms with everything. My mom and my stepmom really like each other and have become good friends. And what makes it so great is that now when they are together we can have fun as a family. Last year we all went skiing together.

Being able to spend time together with both their parents without tension was an important gain noted frequently by children with perfect-pal parents. Debra, a divorced mother with three children, was fifteen when her parents divorced. The oldest of three, she and her siblings agree that their parents were very conflictual for many years after the divorce, but about three or four years ago their relationship really started to improve and has only continued to get better.

> It's strange, because Dad and his wife talk to Mom more than they do to us. Mom and Stewart, my stepdad, are

usually included in some way in Christmas at their house, partly because Dad's mother always comes up for Christmas and she always expects Mom to be around. Things have really improved—in twenty years, they've gotten a lot better, and now they can deal with each other rationally. They actually seem to like each other now. They tease each other and both of them take it, so things have really improved.

Debra's brother adds: "They have an adult relationship now. They couldn't be husband and wife, but they seem to be pretty good friends now. Dad helped my stepdad paint their house last summer." Their younger sister adds wistfully, "It's great to see them get along so well. I just wish they could have gotten to that point when I was younger." Although the children can't pinpoint why the relationship would have changed in recent years, one noted, "I think they have just kind of forgiven a lot of things and everyone has grown up."

Another woman with perfect-pal parents also points to her parents' maturing and coming to terms with some of their marital issues.

I think that they have become more resolved to the divorce and understand more about what was fueling some of the conflict between them. My mom says that she and my dad had a heart-to-heart talk about five years ago when I had surgery and they were able to forgive each other. Ever since then they seem to be best friends.

Cooperative Colleagues

More common than the perfect pals were those parents who the children now described as cooperative colleagues. The paths taken by these parents were varied and complex. Some were angry associates or fiery foes shortly after the divorce, while others were cooperative throughout most of the twenty years since their divorce. But even for the group that maintained a fairly cooperative relationship throughout the years, their children noted some improvement.

Unlike the perfect pals, cooperative colleague parents are not good friends. Some, like Mary's parents, get along very well, but they do not have a relationship separate from their children. "They definitely get along better. They're more driven to help us out, whether that means working together or not. They're very pleasant to each other now and they have no problem spending time with us. The reason I wouldn't call them perfect pals is that they don't talk to each other every week and don't see each other except when we're all together."

Another notes how geographical distance influences their relationship. "I know they e-mail back and forth and talk occasionally. Being so far apart I don't think they see each other very often . . . on holidays and we have Christmas at one place or another. They cross paths and they were both at my wedding and my brother's wedding. They still seem to get along fine."

Holidays, graduations, weddings, and births of grandchildren were the occasions where having parents that get along mattered most. Phillip, now twenty-nine, told us about his sister's recent wedding:

It's really nice now. When we were kids, they still argued a lot, but then when we left home it just seemed to calm down. At my sister's wedding, they all came . . . Dad and my stepmom, and Mom came with Stan, who she's been living with for a year. Everything really went smoothly. They even danced the first dance together. My sister beamed and I felt so glad that they could make this day great for her.

Hilda, his younger sister and the bride, added:

I can't tell you how good it felt to have them all up there with me. Phillip told me not to worry, but I didn't want my wedding spoiled. I mean, I knew they would both come . . . but I didn't know how they would act. But they really seemed to have a good time. Once, I looked over, and Mom was laughing with Dad's mother. They hadn't talked since the divorce!

Paula, an only child who was seven at the time of the divorce, shared this poignant story with us:

For most of my growing-up years, even when they were married, I ran interference between my parents. I even felt guilty that I was the reason that they kept fighting. It got a little better when I was in high school and could make most of the plans myself. The big change happened when I had a baby. It was their first grandchild and they were so excited. I don't know if they made a pact or something but ever since then they've been really okay with each other.

Clearly, being able to have both parents together for special occasions without worrying about whether they would get along brought a sense of relief for many. When parents were able to get along, it increased the adult children's sense of family.

Even twenty years after the divorce, children wanted their parents to have some relationship with each other. As one woman stated,

They have a lot less anger. They are talking to each other now and will exchange information about their health and will ask how each other are doing. They might talk for five minutes or so to each other on the phone when my dad calls for one of us when we're at my mother's house. It makes it so much easier on me to know that they care about each other.

When parents' relationships improved, many children, like Danny, noted that they thought the change came about because the children were now adults.

There was so much anger when they first got divorced. I think they even had a hard time even being near each other. Now they talk once in a while and see each other at family functions and they are always civil and pleasant and fine together. But I think a lot of that had to do with them no longer being in a parenting role.

Another man noted that how his parents now related made it much easier for him to spend time with both of them. He no longer felt the loyalty conflicts that had plagued him in his early years. "They don't argue anymore. They joke around with each other, and are on friendly terms. . . . It is certainly much more humane than it was twenty years ago."

And another woman, Sally, an only child, felt very responsible to keep the peace between her parents. She likes knowing that they can now relate independently of her. "They're doing a lot better. If my mom doesn't hear from me she'll call my dad and ask him what I'm doing."

Angry Associates and Fiery Foes

While over half of those parents who were angry associates or fiery foes shortly after the divorce became cooperative as the years passed, the rest either continued to be conflictual or they stopped talking with each other twenty years later. And their kids talked about how they still felt stressed and angry about it.

"They'll never stop fighting," wailed Jeffrey, who at thirty-one was still distressed about his parents' relationship. "They still complain about each other. You'd think the divorce would have settled some of that." When we asked Jeffrey how it continued to affect his life, he pointed to holidays. "If I go to one of their houses [for Christmas], the other is hurt and angry. Either way I hurt someone, so I just don't go anymore."

Jeffrey's withdrawal from both parents was not unusual for children whose parents were angry associates or fiery foes twenty years after the divorce. It's not that these children didn't want to spend holidays or celebrations with both their parents, but the tension and anticipation of arguments made them either choose between parents or decide to protect themselves by not including either one.

Maggie had this to say:

When my son celebrated his second birthday I invited them both but told them they would have to leave if they fought. They all—Dad's wife was there too—managed to avoid each other for the afternoon but I felt anxious the whole time. I kept watching to make sure they were okay. I'm not sure I would do it that way next time. It takes the fun out it.

Maggie's younger brother Eric, now twenty-nine, made a different decision.

Now that I'm an adult I don't have to put up with their anger any longer. When I got married last year, we decided to have a small wedding and I just invited my mother. I've always been closer to my mother, and she and my dad's wife can't stand the sight of each other. I know my dad was upset but I just told him that's the way it is.

All of the adult children with angry-associate and fiery-foe parents talked about their distress as they tried to maneuver between parents. Weddings, birthdays, graduations were the only times their parents were together and all these occasions posed dilemmas for the children. Some took a hard line and told their parents that they had to be civil or they couldn't participate. Others hoped and prayed their parents would "behave" and not spoil their celebration while still others chose not to involve their parents at all. And still others solved the dilemma by inviting only one parent.

One woman, whose parents have been fiery foes for most of the years since the divorce, was in the midst of planning her wedding. She was still struggling with how to cope with her conflictual parents and protect herself on this special day. "It's a problem. . . . I just want it to be such a beautiful day and I don't want there to be any conflict. I don't want to have to worry about what's going to happen with those two in the same room together. And I'd really love my mom to walk me down the aisle, and everything else. But I also don't know how to tell my dad that I don't want him at my wedding . . . I'm dreading it."

Another woman, Karen, whose parents had been fiery foes since their divorce, made a different choice about her wedding.

We eloped! We got married in Las Vegas, so I didn't have to put up with everyone—and they didn't have to put up with each other. It was the best option, and one we chose I think because of all the conflict in my family.

Some who were single learned from their siblings' weddings that having both parents there ended up spoiling the day. When Melissa was asked to think about the future and what it would be like to plan for a wedding, she talked about her older sister's wedding and had no idea how she would handle her own. "My dad walked out after the ceremony because my stepdad walked my

sister down the aisle. He didn't come to the reception and most of
his family didn't even come to the wedding. The whole reception
was stressful."

Quite a few children told us that it was just easier to keep
their distance from both parents to avoid getting caught in the
cross fire. Stacy, a teenager when her parents divorced, talked of
how she avoided being at home.

> I got really involved in soccer and got on the team. Thank-
> fully, the practices and away games provided me some
> relief. I had a boyfriend and ended up spending a lot of
> time at his house too. They still go at it even now and I
> told them I don't want any part of it. Last week I hung up
> the phone on my mother when she started in on my father.

Those adult children who continued to relate to both parents in
spite of their ongoing hostilities were still plagued with loyalty conflicts. At earlier stages in their lives, some coped with these loyalty
conflicts by siding with one parent or the other. Others felt their
lives were fragmented because they had to keep their relationships
with their parents completely separate. As we saw in chapter 5, relationships with noncustodial fathers were more vulnerable in these
high-conflict families than in the more cooperative ones.

It probably goes without saying at this point, but if divorced
parents want to act "in the best interest of their children," their
best move would be to find some peace with each other. Little is
as stressful to an adult child of divorced parents as parents who
can't be in the same room together without fireworks.

Dissolved Duos

Less than one-fifth of the adult children had parents who they
would characterize as dissolved duos twenty years after the
divorce. These parents disengaged from each other for a number

of different reasons. There were those who slugged it out for many years and then at some point just stopped talking. A few ceased talking within a couple of years after the divorce, and one parent, always the father, withdrew further and further from his children. A few others, again fathers, who were abusive or alcoholic, were court-ordered to have only supervised visitation and, in the words of one of the children, "drifted away" over the years. In a few families, mothers with severe psychological problems caused the children either to distance themselves or to feel burdened by the ongoing relationship.

Some children, even as adults, were still upset and resented their parents. You could hear the anger in Joseph's voice when he spoke about how his parents wavered between being angry associates and fiery foes, and then ended up twenty years later as a dissolved duo.

It went from bad to worse and back again. They couldn't say a civil word to each other. They were just like children. But the worst thing was that they put us in the middle. . . . I hated it when they bad-mouthed each other and my dad expected me to take his side. It got to a point [where] I didn't want to see either of them. Even now they don't talk at all, but it's clear that they still can't stand each other.

Kristen, Joseph's younger sister, was only five when her parents separated, and her voice revealed sadness at the loss of her father.

Oh, my parents don't talk at all anymore and it's a relief. It's better than all the fighting. I haven't seen my dad now for over a year and even before that I only saw him once or twice a year. After he remarried he just seemed to retreat from us more and more. I think the fighting was just too much for him and it was easier not to see us.

About half of this small group with dissolved-duo parents noted that although their parents didn't interact, they both still attended some of their children's special events. "They don't argue, they don't fight, they don't despise each other. They are at the point now where their children are both grown adults so they have no reason to have much contact. They don't call. They don't talk. The only time they see each other now is if there is a function at my brother's or at my place—like at my college graduation, or when my brother had a baby, and then they managed to keep their distance." It was uncomfortable to have both parents present, but for most it was better than leaving one parent out of the picture.

Parents who are simply unable to find any peace with each other after divorce can fairly assume that their children will suffer, at least to some degree, from the sense of fragmentation and the heavy burden of having to plan so carefully for each and every family occasion. The heartening news coming from our study is that even in some of the most contentious divorces, many parents did find ways to become more cooperative as time passed. And their children benefited.

"THESE ARE MY FOLKS": THE OCCASIONS THAT DEFINE YOU AS FAMILY

Ceremonial experiences, like graduations, weddings and births of grandchildren, are opportunities for divorced parents to transform their relationships. Let's be quite clear: Sharing in these events with your children does not require you to be husband and wife. It just requires you to acknowledge your history and the common bond you continue to share. These events, in fact, offer a great opportunity to transform a bad divorce into a good one.

These special occasions also provide opportunities for complex binuclear families to develop their history as family. For children, having their families come together publicly declares to their community and friends the importance of their relationships. It confirms their reality of family. Not only does it give adult children a feeling of wholeness, but it says to all: "These are my folks and they're all here to celebrate with me." It can also be a very important time for acknowledging the role of stepparents and stepkin. The photo albums and videos that will be shown to family, friends and future generations will forever stand as confirmations that you are family.

In fact, it is not uncommon for these public celebrations to be the first occasions where the ex's extended family and the remarried family meet. Marilyn's wedding accomplished this. In spite of very difficult years when her parents seemed to never stop fighting and her stepmother and mother didn't talk to each other, when she got married they all came together.

Everybody came! There were a lot of people from all sides of the family there. My stepmom is a big organizer so she took over during the wedding, getting everyone where they were supposed to be. My stepsisters and my stepbrother were in the bridal party. My "real" mother walked down the aisle with my stepfather and then my brother walked my stepmom down the aisle. My father walked me down the aisle and then he sat in the first pew between my mom and my stepmom. I looked over and saw all four of them sitting there together. I have to tell you it was the greatest feeling seeing all my parents together. If you had told me several years ago that all my parents would be at my wedding and enjoy themselves, I would have said "no way."

Of course these are not always easy occasions. Weddings in particular are likely to unearth old feelings and memories of your own marriage and the circumstances of the divorce. You may be surprised to find that they ignite tender feelings for your ex. Even though you may feel uncomfortable with these feelings, they can help you heal. They will challenge you to move forward, opening the door to improve your divorced parenting relationship.

Your best manners are also called for. Seeing your ex-father-in-law whom you never liked and who hasn't talked to you since the divorce is likely to resurrect old angers. A simple, polite acknowledgment between you may ease the tension of years of held resentments.

MORE THAN ENOUGH
LOVE TO GO AROUND

Weddings can also open up overlapping and often sensitive relationship issues. Rachel lived primarily with her mother and was seven when her mother remarried Howard. Over the years she developed a close and loving relationship with him. Although her father lived several hundred miles away she saw him monthly, talked with him frequently and spent part of her summers with him and his remarried family. Although Rachel had no immediate plans for marriage, she did have some ideas—and anxieties—about how she would like her wedding to be.

> I think it would be fine. The only part would be walking me down the aisle, and I have already decided. I would have to have both of my dads—my dad and my stepdad— walk me down. I would *have* to have both. I couldn't possibly choose one. Biologically my dad is my dad, but emotionally my stepdad is my dad, too. I know my stepdad would accept that, and my dad would have to, and I think he probably would.

The fact is, parenting isn't just a matter of biology but of the roles people play in the lives of children. Rachel's stepfather was very much a father to her, and Rachel's desire to have both of her fathers share this wedding tradition clearly establishes this. Allowing for healthy bonding to occur in binuclear families challenges our traditional notions of family, but the reality is that the members of these extended tribes *are* your children's family. It may feel threatening to you if your children form a close bond with a stepparent, but that love does not diminish their love for you. When parents embrace this, children are not only freed from painful loyalty conflicts, they can also experience the real advantages of having several parents to love and be loved by, additional adults who can support, nurture and guide them. There may be few perks to divorce, but this is definitely one of them.

EVERLASTING BONDS

If you are a parent in the midst of divorce and you have young children it may feel difficult to peek into your future, but rest assured that the relationship you have with your exspouse will have a rippling effect on the meaningful bonds of family. There are many losses that accompany divorce but the loss of family does not have to be one of them.

When parents are cooperative throughout the years, their children's potential for troubles are reduced substantially. Children continue to have relationships with both parents, financial support usually continues and children experience fewer disruptions to their lives. They retain the security and connection that comes from having a family. As adults these children show no ill effects from their parents' divorce and often experience some unexpected gains from living in a binuclear family.

But even if parents are not cooperative to begin with but become more amicable over the years, families can still survive and children can thrive. As we have seen thus far, how children respond to the changes in their families after divorce depends in large part on the strengths of their parents. But it is only when we add the personal attributes of the child, his or her resilience in the face of stressful changes, and their economic circumstances that we get a fuller picture of the long-term effects of divorce. As we will see in the next chapter, even when they do not have parents who can manage to get along, there are other paths that some children find that help them grow into healthy adults.

Part Three

Strengthening Our Binuclear Families

Chapter 8

FOSTERING RESILIENCE

Helping Children Thrive in Their Postdivorce Families

You don't have to be a rocket scientist to know that some divorces are easier on kids than others. Throughout this book we've been gathering information from adult children of divorce about the things parents can do not only to minimize the stress of divorce but to help their children thrive in the postdivorce family. If we were to prescribe the winning formula it would look something like this:

- be supportive and nurturing
- don't involve the kids in your conflicts
- stay involved in their lives
- respect each other's rights as parents
- communicate with each other about the children's needs
- provide a stable and secure family environment

But, as we all know, what works as an ideal can be an awfully tall order in real life. For example, I can tell you that it's better for your child not to have to move from the family home, and you will tell me that you can't afford to keep the house. I can tell you to keep your child in the same school, and you will tell me that you have to move to an apartment and there are no multiple-family dwellings in that school district. I can tell you that it's important that your child's father stay involved, and you will tell me that his father moved 250 miles away and can't see the kids very often. I can tell you that it's best that you don't fight with your ex, especially in front of the kids, and you will tell me that it's your ex who won't let go, who won't stop fighting, who sabotages every visit. Fortunately, children don't need ideal circumstances to thrive, and no parent should be made to feel guilty that she isn't able to meet all the criteria. Having an ideal, however, does provide a model to aim toward and a guidepost for promoting healthy families after divorce.

WHAT MAKES A FAMILY STRONG?

With its disruption to the daily routines and rituals of family life, divorce inevitably thrusts parents and children into a state of limbo. The key to surviving the transition, both for parents and children, is resilience. It is resilience that allows us to successfully manage stressful changes—the ability to bounce back from adversity, to face a crisis with the resources to adapt. Resilient people are able to use whatever resources they have to protect them in times of distress. Resilience also explains how some children overcome difficult obstacles while others become victims of their early experiences.

Although we commonly think about resilience as an extraordinary trait that some people just have, the reality is that we all have the capacity to be resilient and every one of us encounters some adversity in our lives that requires us to be resilient. It has its roots in childhood experiences and the skills we learned then to help us cope. Some of us may be more resilient than others, but it is certainly not a fixed trait. It is something we learn, and it can be taught. If your children are showing signs of distress, helping them foster resilience can be one of the most important things you do and this chapter will give you some pointers.

The best thing we can do to help our children develop their own capacity for resilience is to prepare them well.

When and How to Break the News

If you haven't yet told your children you are divorcing, decisions about when, how and what to tell them probably weigh heavily on your mind. In my clinical practice, these are among the most common questions parents ask me. How much in advance should we tell the children? Should we both tell them? What should we tell them? Parents are very concerned about upsetting their children and worry about how they will respond. Sometimes this worry causes them either not to tell the children or to wait until the last minute—sometimes the actual day of the separation—to break the news.

The interviews with the adult children offered up a number of important tips for parents who are considering or about to divorce:

1) *Consider your child's age and temperament when deciding how soon to tell.* Young children have little conception of time and shouldn't be given much advance notice. Older children often pick up that something is wrong and would prefer to be told directly and given some time to deal with it before the actual separation occurs.

It's important to know that, except for young children (those under seven), children usually remember being told. And how they're told matters—a lot. Some have such vivid memories that they can remember where they were sitting, what they were wearing, how their parents looked, the words their parents spoke. Others have only a vague memory of being told.

As the children in the study talked about how they were told, *all felt that it was important to tell children and to do so well before the actual separation.* Children want to be told, and when they aren't they resent it. It makes them more confused and anxious when they don't know what's happening and don't have the time to prepare for what's ahead.

When a separation happens suddenly and it's not possible to tell the children in advance, the best you can do is try to help them feel secure. If they had no idea it was coming (which is often not the case), they will likely feel bewildered and perhaps frightened. Young children especially may need to be reassured frequently that you will not leave them.

2) *If at all possible, decide beforehand, with your spouse, what you are going to tell your children and sit down together to share the news.* Children don't want or need all the dirty details. What they need is to know that their parents have made the decision and have thought through what will happen next.

I realize this is not always possible. For example, an angry spouse may sabotage the situation by telling the children in order to illicit their support or punish the spouse. All you can do in that case is to patch up the damage done and reassure the children that they are loved and will be taken care of, in spite of their parents' anger or distress with each other.

3) *Talk to your kids about how their lives will change, how they will be cared for, where they will live and how they will continue to see both parents.* Children are most concerned with their day-to-day needs and most are very fearful of the change. Over and over again, the children told us how important it was for them to have the chance to talk to their parents and be part of the plan that was going to affect their lives.

Kids today are surrounded by divorce and it is a rare child who doesn't know another child with divorced parents. Based on their limited knowledge they form their own views of what happens when parents divorce. They know, for instance, that Tony down the street spends some weekends with his father or Kelly has a stepmother. Others will have friends who are sad or unhappy because they don't see their father and others who brag about the two Christmas holidays and all the extra presents they get. Older children are most concerned about how the divorce will interrupt their lives, whether they will have to move or babysit for the younger sibs more frequently, or what their friends will think of them.

4) *Give your children time to process the news.* Whenever any of us undergoes a life transition, it helps to know what to expect. It's no wonder that books about what to expect as we transition to a new and unknown stage in our lives are so popular. The mother who is tearing her hair out because her two-year-old refuses to listen to her grabs today's version of Dr. Spock on her bedside table and sighs with relief as she reads that it is developmentally appropriate for her child to be rebellious. She then reads ahead to the next chapter dealing with the age of three and goes to sleep hopeful that she can look forward to her obstinate child becoming more mellow, desiring once again to please. So it is with your kids. They want to know what to expect, and you can help them a great deal by being prepared to answer this question.

It is worth noting here that one of the universal truths about divorce is that children don't really care when a divorce becomes legal or official. As far as they're concerned the marker event is the day one parent moves out.

5) *Explore with your children what they know about divorce and what they think and fear will happen.* Many children ask concrete questions, and if parents have made plans for how and

exactly when the separation will take place, it helps children feel more secure. If parents do not yet know the specifics they need to reassure their children that they will continue to take good care of them and will let them know as the plans get formed. Children want to know that even though things are changing, their parents can be depended on to keep them safe.

6) *Listen to your kids, but don't make them choose whom to live with.* In custody issues that are brought to the courts for resolution, children under twelve are not customarily consulted, but children over twelve usually do get to voice their choice about which parent they want to live with. Many of the older children who make these choices are haunted by loyalty conflicts afterward. They would have preferred not to have had to make the choice and often resented that they were put in that position.

If the anger and retaliation are such that you cannot make decisions about custody and living arrangements, get professional help as soon as possible. Find someone to mediate your dispute—a counselor, mediator, parent coordinator, minister or rabbi, friend, relative. Having a court custody battle has no positive outcomes. Everyone loses, especially the children.

But what about parents who are too angry with each other, too distraught themselves to be able to sit down with their children and have this very emotional and distressing talk? And what if the separation happens quickly, perhaps on the heels of a bad fight or a betrayal just discovered? In these situations, *when parents are unable to tell their children without inflicting their own rage or depression, they need to find someone who can tell the children and listen to their needs.* A grandparent, close friend, or sibling may be willing to talk to the children and help them cope better with the news. When parents have better control of their own emotions, they can then sit down and talk with the children themselves.

Therapists can be very helpful at these times. Family sessions provide a safe place for you and your children to talk about the divorce and the impending consequences. When I consult with families in these early stages I have found that it brings parents and children closer together. It is empowering for families to problem-solve together about how best to manage the difficult changes facing them.

It is worth repeating here that divorce is one of many choices parents make in their lives when their needs and the children's may be in conflict. Except in the most highly conflictual and abusive marital situations, children want to live with *both* of their parents. Parents need to expect that no matter how well they present it, their children will initially be angry, sad or disappointed.

What to Say About Why

Intertwined with breaking the news comes the decision about what to say about *why* you're divorcing. Most children are told that their parents are divorcing because they're "incompatible," aren't getting along or are unhappy with each other. Older children often have more knowledge or insight about what's really causing the divorce but are usually quite satisfied with the stock response about incompatibility.

Whether or not they know the cause from the start, they will usually develop their own ideas as they mature and as new information filters in. If, for example, your child discovers that you had been having an affair, naturally her assessment of what caused your divorce will change accordingly. If your children become aware that you were already involved with a partner you later married, they will, likewise, put two and two together.

One fear especially common in young children whose parents have divorced is that if their parents could stop loving each other then they can also stop loving them. Young children need frequent reassurance that their parents will *never* stop loving them even when they do bad things.

Children need to be reassured that they are not to blame. If you tended to argue about the kids within their earshot, or if your kids were a "problem," they're particularly susceptible to blaming themselves for the divorce—and particularly in need of reassurance that they didn't cause it. It is a heavy burden for children when they feel like they caused their parents to split up. Even if they later realize that this wasn't the case, it is important to give them the message, early and often, that they are not to blame.

Some parents, particularly mothers who are angry at being left by their husbands, will say, even against their better judgment, "Daddy left *us*," and when their child asks the inevitable "why," the mother will respond with something like, "Because Daddy doesn't love *us* anymore." No matter how tempting that may be, it is so important not to do that. It can leave children wondering for a very long time what they did to cause Daddy to leave or stop loving them. It also makes them feel as if they are unlovable. You might want to explain to your children, as appropriate to their age, that the love between adults is very different from the love that parents have for their kids. This can help put them at ease.

So much for determining when and how and what to say. Now let's take a look at how children cope with the multiple changes that commonly occur for years after.

PREDICTABLE CHANGES

There is no question that marital separation, no matter what the state of the marriage, sets off a unique series of dramatic and abrupt transitions that can stress even the most adaptable child. As we have seen in earlier chapters, divorce may mean moving to a new home or splitting their time between two different homes, or changing schools and leaving friends, or having a parent move two towns away, or having less money to live on. Down the road it often means seeing their parents with a new love, some stranger who may even come to live with them and act like a parent, new sisters and brothers whom they may or may not get along with, and inevitably more changes in how and where they live.

Let's consider the following list of the twelve most common transitions experienced by children after divorce. Although many of these changes have been discussed in earlier chapters, here our focus will shift to their *cumulative* effects and how to avoid full-blown crises and reduce children's distress over the short and long term. Each one of these changes can create serious disruptions in a child's life, and even those that may appear to parents as positive gains can feel like losses to a child at the time. Of course not all children will experience all these changes, but most have to adapt to at least some of them.

- Moving and geographical changes
- School changes
- Downturn in living standards
- Changes in custody and living arrangements
- Mother's remarriage(s)
- Father's remarriage(s)
- Gaining stepsiblings from a stepfather
- Gaining stepsiblings from a stepmother
- Mother's new baby (half sibling)
- Father's new baby (half sibling)
- A mother's second divorce
- A father's second divorce

Some people flow more easily with change than others. Think about it. Perhaps you lived in one house in one town or city for all of your childhood years. You might have always yearned to break free or you may have liked the predictability and stability and become rather fearful or wary of change. Perhaps you were from a military or corporate family and moved many times during childhood. Again, that might have taught you to be very adaptable and to view change as a normal part of life, or you might have become anxious about moving and still find it terribly debilitating. These differences show up pretty early in life.

This is not to suggest that if you have an anxious child you shouldn't move on with your life. But even if you have the most adventurous children, a certain amount of stability in the first few years will make the transition easier. As we saw earlier, the more we help children to anticipate and prepare for the changes, with knowledge about what to expect, the easier those changes will be. It is always easier for children to adapt if transitions don't come too rapidly or too many at one time. For example, it is very helpful for children not to have to make an immediate geographical move or change schools. Although economics often require that the family home be sold, parents should try their best to put that off for at least a year to provide some stability while the children are adjusting to living in two households.

Let's look at how too many changes too soon affected a few children. Tammy was seven, the youngest of three, when her parents separated. Sad and confused, she missed the daily contact with her father and looked forward to seeing him on Wednesday evenings and two or three weekends a month. When he moved in with his future wife and her two children shortly after the divorce, Tammy felt like she was not as important to him anymore. Although she continued to see her father one evening a week and a couple of weekends a month, she felt like she had to share him with another family.

"I hated having to go to *her* house to be with my father. It was like he was snatched from me. I remember he told me that he loved me just as much as he used to, but I didn't believe him. I felt like he had traded me in, abandoned me for his new family. I used to wish they would all die so I could have my daddy back.

Tammy never completely recovered from her distress about her father's remarriage and saw him less and less over the years. As an adult she felt strongly that had he not jumped into a new relationship with new kids so quickly, she might have had fewer problems.

As Joel, who was eleven when his parents divorced, remembers back to that time, he says it was like "bombs seemed to be going off every few weeks." His parents sold the house during the divorce proceedings and he and his father moved to one apartment, and his two sisters and his mother to another. He saw his sisters on Saturdays and his mother once or twice a week. Six months later his father moved again, and Joel had to change schools for a second time. Adjusting to not living full-time with his mother and his sisters was difficult. Compounding these losses the two moves and new schools meant he had to give up friendships and the security of a familiar neighborhood. It should come as no surprise that within two years of the divorce, Joel's grades dropped and teachers reported that he was aggressive and rebellious.

As he remembers it,

I was a really angry kid. I didn't have any friends for a couple of years. As I look back now I can see how scared I was and how much I missed my sisters and my mother. A year later, I ran away and then I moved back in with my mother.

Shannon had a different experience. She was nine when her parents separated and her father moved to a town house less than a mile away. She spent half the week with her mother and the other half with her father.

> It was a little strange at first but I got used to it and I felt luckier than some other kids who only saw their fathers on Saturdays. They both came to my softball games, and if I forgot something at the other house I could go back and get it. It was different, and I remember that sometimes I felt sad, but mostly it worked out fine. They were really good about not fighting and I knew I was very important to both of them.

Shannon's father remarried two years later and moved with his new wife and her five-year-old son to a larger house a half mile away. Six months later he and Shannon's mother decided to change Shannon's living schedule from half weeks to alternating weeks with each parent.

> At first I remember worrying about whether Sylvia and her son James would mean my father wouldn't have as much time for me, but that didn't happen. It was fun to have a little brother. He wasn't there most weekends because he was with his dad. That gave me special time alone with my dad.

Although Shannon had to cope with several transitions over the first few years, she had sufficient time to adapt to each of them individually. Her father's remarriage might have created more problems for her if it had resulted in her seeing less of him, but because her relationships with her parents remained stable throughout she didn't experience the distress often associated with loss.

When transitions happen quickly and pile up one upon another, you can expect your children to feel overwhelmed.

While they might be able to cope effectively with moving to a new neighborhood and school shortly after the divorce, if they also have to adapt to a new stepparent at the same time, it may be more change than they can handle. It bears repeating: Too many changes too soon will diminish the coping capacities of even the most resilient children.

It takes two parents working together in the children's best interests to discuss the impact of each of their lifestyle changes. When parents can't do this, however, each will have to deal independently with their children's distress about the family changes. For example, if your ex has remarried and your children are unhappy, it would be helpful for you to try to help them adapt to the situation. If you are angry or jealous it is very seductive to want to agree with the children when they come to you, as they are likely to do, with their complaints. It's important that you try to separate their best interests from your own anger. Helping them to understand that it's only natural that they will need time to feel comfortable with a new adult in their lives will go a long way toward helping them better cope.

If, after serious thought and perhaps some consultation with a professional, you think your children really have some serious cause for their distress, like an abusive stepparent or irresolvable personality conflicts, then you may want to take some steps to alleviate it. Perhaps changing their living arrangements, even on a temporary basis, will improve their situation. Unfortunately, if you and your ex can't communicate, this may very likely escalate to a custody battle that will create more distress for your children.

Clearly, coparenting after divorce is the best solution to helping children cope effectively with the difficult changes. It's not that parents can alleviate all the stress of the cumulative changes, but together they can buffer its impact.

BUFFERS

Fortunately there are many buffers that can help minimize the impact of stressful situations on kids. Friends, neighbors, church or school activities can help a child through difficult periods. A child's age, gender, birth order, temperament, intelligence and physical appearance also contribute to their ability to be flexible and adaptable, to be resilient. As we saw in chapter 3, the dynamics of the predivorce family, and especially of the parents' marital relationship, weighs heavily in predisposing children to their responses to divorce-related stresses. Likewise, the best buffer against the potential risks of divorce is two loving parents who shield their children from their parents' conflicts.

That having been said and with the knowledge that at least half of all divorces do not end up with this best-case scenario, let's take a look at how children utilize other buffers to cope effectively with their distress.

Same Divorce, Different Reactions

Throughout this book I have noted that siblings often respond and cope differently with their parents' divorce. What may have been upsetting for one child is simply not a major problem for another. One child may have a good relationship with a stepparent, while her brother doesn't. One sibling might blame his mother for the dissolution of the marriage, another his father. What appears to be the same divorce from the outside is often not the same at all within the family.

Although siblings in all families will have differing takes on how their family history affected their lives, some sibling differences are more extreme than others. What I found in my study is that the more the parents' conflicts dominate the family, the more intensely the siblings will differ in feelings and memories about the marriage and divorce. These differences also affected relation-ships *between* siblings—their relationships were not as close as those siblings who grew up with more cooperative parents. Clearly, the effects of destructive conflict between parents, and the divided loyalties that usually result, have deep roots with branches that spread into other areas of family functioning.

Let's take a close look at how differently the siblings in one family were affected by their parents' divorce:

Carrie, Leslie and Peter

Carrie, the eldest of three children, was fourteen when her parents separated.

"I remember my father taking me on a drive and telling me that my mom had served him papers and that he had to move out. I was really angry at my mother for breaking up our family. I remember crying and asking him why and all he said was that she was unhappy with him."

Carrie's two younger siblings, Leslie and Peter, had a different picture of their parents' breakup. Leslie, age eleven at the time, remembers her mother sitting at the kitchen table with her and her nine-year-old brother, Peter, and tearfully telling them that she and their dad were going to get a divorce. "Peter didn't say much but I was kind of relieved. I mean, I felt sad, but I also felt like it was the best thing. My father drank a lot, and when he did he got very mean. We were all scared of him when he came home drunk but I think it was the worst for me. I don't know why but he just yelled and hit me more than he did Carrie or Peter.

Peter remembers being scared and asking his mother where they would all live.

"I was sad but I wasn't too surprised because they yelled and screamed a lot and it wasn't very happy at home anymore. I remember asking my mom if I caused it because I used to fight with my sisters a lot and she told me over and over that they both loved all of us and that we were the best part of their marriage."

A few days later their father moved out to an apartment only a few blocks away. Although the children stayed in the family home with their mother, this arrangement didn't last very long. Only a few weeks after their dad moved out, Carrie followed. "I couldn't stand living with my mother. We had never gotten along really well and the fights only got worse. I don't even remember what the fight was about but she slapped me and I ran out of the house and ran crying to my grandparents. I stayed with them for a few days and then I moved in with my dad."

Their parents' divorce was acrimonious and the court ordered a custody evaluation. Carrie remembers saying she wanted to live with her dad and Leslie remembers that she wanted to live with her mom. About a year later, the court awarded their parents split custody with flexible visiting arrangements. Carrie and Peter were to live with their father, Leslie with her mother. The children were to spend weekends together at one or the other of their parents' homes. Only Peter remembers feeling upset with this decision. "I felt okay about living with my dad, mainly because he moved back into the house and my mother and Leslie moved out to an apartment. But then I felt badly about my mom and worried a lot about her not having enough money. Going back and forth was always hard. I always felt split and like I was hurting my mom's feelings." All three children remember a lot of arguments between their parents during these first few years but only Leslie remembers feeling caught in the middle. "I think I got the brunt of it because I was the one who wanted to be with my mom and I didn't like going to be with my dad. My mother would make me go and my father knew I didn't want to be there and he blamed my mother. It was a mess."

Peter managed to keep good relationships with both sisters, although he felt closer to Carrie. "She was like a mother to me.

Dad worked a lot and she cooked and took care of me and I always felt real close to her." Carrie and Leslie didn't have a good relationship before the divorce, but both felt it got worse afterward. "I resented Carrie a lot for going to live with Dad. I knew that she was always his favorite. Whenever anything came up I took Mom's side and she took Dad's."

When the children reflected on how the divorce affected their lives, each had a different perspective. Carrie feels she "became a stronger person. I was a caretaker because I had to take care of my brother a lot. Even though I resented it at times I think it gave me a sense of responsibility and a feeling of being needed. My mom and I still don't get along real well. She's more like a friend maybe than a mother. I consider my grandmother to be more of a mother. Maybe like a surrogate mother." Now married for nine years, Carrie has two children and a stepson who visits for a couple of weeks in the summer.

Peter feels that, as the youngest and the only boy, the divorce "took its toll. I felt lonely and wished I had a brother. I spent most weekends with my mom and talked to her every day. Although I liked living with my dad I could talk with my mom about more things and feel closer to her. When I got to high school I know I was saved from getting into a lot of trouble by being good at sports. Basketball became my life. My coach was a great man, my model, and I'm still close with him." Peter joined the navy right after high school and says, "That's when I really grew up. There was a chaplain I got really close to and he helped me get my head on straight. When I got out of the service I went back to live with Dad while I went to college and it was a good time for us. I really got to know him then. My mother was happier and financially better off after she remarried and I enjoy spending time with them." Peter got married just recently to his high school girlfriend. "One thing the divorce taught me was to be very careful about marriage. I wanted to wait until I was thirty and I almost made it! I don't drink at all because of my dad's problem and I really know I want to try to be a better husband than my dad was."

Leslie's adolescence was much more turbulent than her siblings'. Although her mother was dating, it wasn't until Leslie was fifteen that her mother became involved in a serious relationship. "Until Ted came along I was pretty happy just living with my mom and we spent a lot of time together, just my mom and me. Then Ted moved in and everything changed. I started to hang with a group of wild kids, drank a lot, tried some drugs and fought with my mom whenever she tried to control me. It was a bad time, and when I was not quite eighteen I got pregnant and ran off and got married. That lasted only a couple of years and then I came home with my daughter and lived with my mom and Ted for a while. The next couple of years were bad. I hadn't gone to college like Carrie or Peter and worked as a waitress part-time. I was drinking and staying out and my mom gave me the ultimatum: either I shape up or get out. She said I had to go to counseling or I couldn't stay there. It was the best thing that happened to me."

Leslie remarried a couple of years ago and feels good about her life now. She has joint custody with her daughter's father and encourages their time together. She feels it took her a while to grow up and that her mother's remarriage had more of a negative effect on her than the divorce did. "It was just more than I could cope with at the time and I really didn't know where to turn. I felt like I lost my mother and I didn't have Carrie either."

All three siblings report that after more than a decade of being angry associates, their parents have finally "buried the hatchet" and actually get along quite well now. So well, in fact, that they even celebrate some holidays together as a family. Says Carrie, "It has a lot to do with my stepfather. He and my dad get along really well. But as bad as things sometimes got I have to credit my parents with always loving us kids and trying to do the best by us."

Although this was an unusual custody arrangement because it

split the siblings between parents, many children end up with informal arrangements that are similar. If you remember, in chapter 4, we found that over half of the children changed their living arrangements some years after the divorce. Often it was only one child in a family that moved from one parent's home to another, and often it was initiated because of a parent's remarriage.

Carrie and Peter both had buffers that helped them thrive during difficult and stressful times. Carrie was close with her paternal grandmother and Peter had a good relationship with both of his sisters and his mother, then later on with his coach. Leslie, the middle child, did not have such buffers. Her major resource was her mother, and when her mother became less available to her she had trouble coping. Had she been able to turn for emotional support to her father or another adult at that time, she would have had a better chance of coping more effectively with the changes in her mother's life.

Carrie's role in the family was what psychologists call a "parentified child." During her teen years she became the little adult to her brother and father. Parentified children take on adult responsibilities at the expense of not getting their own developmental needs met. They grow up too quickly. Although Carrie often resented her family responsibilities, as an adult she felt it helped her become independent and strong. A positive outcome was that she was a resource to her younger brother and they formed a close relationship that continued into adulthood. Close relationships between siblings help them feel less vulnerable and often counterbalance the stresses of parental discord.

Peter, by putting his energies into his high school basketball team, was able to escape the distress he felt at home. He gained self-esteem through his sports achievements and the close relationship he developed with his coach. Positive school experiences help children, especially during their preadolescent and adolescent years, navigate the risks of stressful family situations and develop important life skills.

Leslie was the child who felt the most negative impact of her parents' dysfunctional marriage and subsequent divorce. She identified with her mother and even before the separation she had a difficult time with her father. She describes herself as a shy child, very attached to her mother, who felt jealous of her sister's more outgoing personality and her closeness with their grandparents. During her adolescence, when her mother recoupled, she felt abandoned. Lacking the resilience and access to the healthy resources that either of her siblings had, she floundered and found acceptance from a peer group of similarly troubled teens. Turning to alcohol and drugs as a way to dull the pain of her distress, she became pregnant in her late teens. When children's needs are unmet it can generate more problems, hence increasing the risks in their lives. Such was the case with Leslie.

In her mid-twenties Leslie hit "rock bottom" and reached a "turning point." Divorced and with a young child, at her mother's insistence she sought counseling. With several years of counseling, her mother and stepfather's support and her second marriage to a responsible and loving man, she was able to accept herself and gain enough self-confidence to lead a happier and more satisfying life. Her relationship with her father and siblings improved as well, so much so that they have all spent several holidays together in the past couple of years. She regrets not getting a college education like her siblings did and she is now thinking of remedying that by applying to a nearby community college. Twenty years after her parents' divorce, at age thirty-one, she is leading a reasonably happy life but the stresses of her earlier years have left their mark.

These siblings, like many others, have different capacities for resilience. They had different temperaments, were at different stages in their development and each used environmental and familial resources differently. It is also likely that their birth order and gender contributed to their differences.

In most families with two or more children, differences in resilience between siblings are common. In some situations there are extreme differences, such as the case of two brothers, one who became a very successful professional and the other who dropped out of school and continues to have troubles with the law. Or another family with four siblings, two who continue to be troubled as adults by their parents' divorce while the other two siblings are living happy, productive lives. Although it is never possible to identify all the factors that combine to make siblings different, we can see from these examples how siblings each experience their parents' divorce differently and how their individual strengths and limitations affect how they cope. It should be clear from this one example that we cannot assume that divorce has similar effects on all the children in a family—just another reminder that generalized conclusions simply don't have much value as we assess whether or when or how to divorce.

Similarly, we cannot understand divorce's impact by looking at children at only one point in time. What we discover about how a child is functioning one year after divorce, for example, won't necessarily apply a year or two or ten later. At the time of the divorce and for a year or two afterward, when their parents were still engaged in a custody dispute, Carrie would have looked like the most troubled of the three siblings. At that time, she was the angriest and most distressed of the three children. Five years after the divorce, and even at ten years, Leslie clearly would have fit the picture of a highly troubled teenager and young adult, while Carrie would have shown no indicators of long-term damage. Our brief look at these three siblings is sufficient to tell us how misleading the findings from these studies may be.

A third problem, as chapter 3 clearly shows, occurs when we attribute a child's dysfunction to a parental divorce without accounting for the effects of the predivorce years. Leslie fits a number of common criteria used by researchers to identify children who were seriously damaged by their parents' divorce. She got married early, was pregnant prior to the marriage, didn't achieve academically, and got divorced herself.

Would she have had these problems if her parents had stayed married? Although it's not possible to know the answer to the question, we do know that before the divorce Leslie was less resilient in coping with life's stresses than her siblings. She was more withdrawn, had fewer environmental resources to draw upon, and because of her close identification with her mother she got more of her father's anger than her siblings did.

Leslie believes her parents' fighting and her father's drinking and abuse would have made her life much worse. The research supports her. Children living in high-conflict "intact" families have been found to suffer more ill effects than children whose parents divorced. Although her parents continued to be in conflict for many years afterward, Leslie feels she was better off not having to live with it on a daily basis. Twenty years later, by her own assessment, she feels she is better off because of the divorce. She feels her life is now on track and rated herself as average on our measures of well-being.

Not All Children Thrive

It's a sad fact of life that some children simply do not have the resilience to overcome the extreme adversity in their lives. Even though we can point to well-known figures like Antwone Fisher and Oprah Winfrey as examples of people who succeed in spite of their misfortunes, the silent majority are those children who do not. These children become victims of their environments.

As adults, one-fifth of the children in this study had serious problems. They were unhappy in their personal lives as well as their work lives. Some were single, longing to find an intimate relationship, others were unhappily married and still others had been married and divorced at least once. On our measures of well-being they rated themselves as below average in self-esteem, success and happiness. Most had poor relationships with their parents, stepparents and siblings. Many blamed the divorce, their parents' marriage, or a dysfunctional parent for their difficulties.

In some ways the pieces to the puzzle fit together more easily when describing the children who are victims than it does for those who show no long-term ill effects. There were striking similarities in these children's family histories. Many had parents who were themselves dysfunctional. These were the mothers or fathers who had histories of emotional problems and who, when we interviewed them, were depressed or highly anxious. The incidence of alcohol, drug and physical abuse was also much higher in this group of families. Many of these participants were products of high-conflict marriages and divorces, and had lost or never had a relationship with their fathers. Almost all of the children in this group had reduced economic circumstances as a result of the divorce.

A few had stepparents who were alcoholic or who physically or sexually abused them. Some had irresolvable personality conflicts with stepparents and had no other parent or family to escape to. Some shifted back and forth between parents and never felt like either parent wanted them.

In spite of overwhelming odds, some children in these families were highly resilient. Brent, one of the children in this group, reflected on how he managed not to succumb to the unfortunate circumstances he grew up in. "It was a lousy childhood. I wouldn't wish it on anyone. I can't even remember a time when I felt safe at home. But, you know, you just have to take what life sends your way and do your best to climb out of that hole. I figured the best way to do that was to work real hard in school, and I used to hang out down at the community center a lot so I wouldn't have to go home. I used to do my homework there." A woman, Maria, said that her religious beliefs helped her survive. "I prayed a lot and joined the children's choir at the church. A lot of people there were very nice to me and made me feel like I was important. I know that helped me decide that I could make it in this world if

I just kept trying." Her brother, Wayne, was not as fortunate. "I was too messed up. A kid just can't make it if their father walks out and their mother sleeps around."

Would these children have been better off if their parents had stayed together? Although a few wished their parents were still together, most felt their lives would not have been any better and some felt that it would even have been worse. These children were dealt a bad hand, not *just* because their parents had divorced, but because their parents were not competent or capable of meeting their children's needs. In some cases, the divorce perpetuated their unfortunate circumstances. In some cases, the divorce made their living situations worse. Not only did these children lack good parenting but they also lacked environmental and internal resources that could have improved their lives. Most felt stuck. They lacked sufficient inner strength to change their lives.

There were some siblings in these families, however, who overcame their histories and went on to have more fulfilling lives. They are the survivors, the ones who thrived. They rarely did it alone, however. They usually found someone in their lives who believed in them, and through that support they gained the courage to improve their lives. They were active participants in their own lives, optimistic about their capacity to overcome their adversity.

Looking at how siblings differ is further evidence that there are no easy answers. Understanding and predicting how a parental divorce will affect any individual child is complex and as we have seen depends on a wide range of factors. Looking at real children and how they thrive after divorce, however, reveals ways in which parents can minimize the risks. It also identifies pitfalls to try to avoid. Each parent, and each family, then has to apply these to their own situation and each of their children's developmental needs.

Even though this group of at-risk children represents only a minority of children who experience a parental divorce, it still gives us reason for serious concern. The current divorce rates indicate that over one million children experience the divorce of their parents annually. Twenty percent of those children is approximately 200,000 children annually that are at high risk for long-term problems. This compares with about 10 to 15 percent of children who did *not* experience divorce and who are also considered high-risk. Of course, although it is not possible to eliminate all the societal and family problems that put children at risk (such as poverty, which is a major contributor), by understanding and applying some principles of resilience we can at least try to help children cope more effectively. Understanding why some children thrive while others do not is a step in that direction.

Increasing Your Child's Resilience

Although a supportive coparenting relationship is the best buffer against the stresses of divorce, when that is not possible parents can still continue to be good parents. In many situations destructive conflicts can be avoided if parents have little or no interaction. Although this kind of *parallel* parenting is more difficult for both children and their parents, it is a better solution than the loss of one parent.

Especially for young children, a nurturing and supportive relationship with at least one parent helps buffer some of the risks of divorce. Suzanne was nine when her parents divorced. It was a stormy separation, and several months after the divorce her father took a new job that required him to move several hundred miles away. Suzanne had been close with her father and was sad and distressed about seeing him infrequently. "I had a hard time of it and I know I was a difficult kid. If it wasn't for my mother I don't know how I would have turned out. I don't know how she managed to do it, but no matter what crap was going on in her life, she was there for me." Many of the others in the study also credited their mothers as being the person who most helped them to cope with the stresses of the divorce. Researchers who study resilience conclude that the guidance of a strong, responsive and nurturing parent offers children one of the most important protective buffers.

Mothers fill this role more often than fathers, both in marriage and after divorce, but fathers should not overlook their child's needs for his parenting. Even if a child's primary home is with her mother, fathers who are consistently supportive and available can provide a child with the stability, security and parental guidance that help her develop into a well-functioning adult. A reminder to fathers: Even when you can't see your children as much as you might like, being consistent and letting them know that you care will help build their self-esteem. It's important for your children to know that you will be there if they need you. During their adolescent years, when children are establishing their needs for independence, relationships with their parents often become adversarial. If they live with their mother most of the time, she is likely to be the parent who is the target of their rebellion. Fathers can be an important resource at that time and many children find that moving in with their fathers, even temporarily, reduces some of the immediate stress.

Other Buffers

Other adults can also help children navigate stressful times. Grandparents or other extended family members, even neighbors and family friends, can help protect and guide children during stressful times. Friendships are very important to adolescents and a special friend is often the one who helps them get through rough periods.

It's important that we not overlook stepparents as another possible source of support. As we saw in chapter 6, some children found stepparents to be substitute parents, others found them to be bonus parents and still others turned to them as friends. A good relationship with a stepparent can become a child's safety zone. They can often talk about things with their stepparent that they're not able to with their parents. Stepparents find that if they tread lightly and develop a trusting relationship with their stepchild, they will often be able to help them through some rough spots.

Children benefit from as many supportive adult relationships as they can get. When parents are too absorbed by their own difficulties, children gain immeasurably by having another adult to turn to and seek guidance from. Erik, eight when his parents divorced, thanks his mother for her resourcefulness. "She knew I was really upset about not seeing my dad and she found me a 'big brother.' To this day, I thank her for knowing what I needed and then making sure I got it." Other children benefited from relationships with coaches, teachers, or school counselors. The point is, parents can steer their children toward outside resources. It's a wise and resilient parent who knows how and when to seek outside support to help meet her children's needs.

How Children Can Help Themselves

By now it's become quite clear that even twenty years after divorce, conflictual parents continue to create difficult situations for their adult children. Learning to cope with these situations requires grown-up children to take active steps to increase their own resilience. Taking a lead from those children who overcame difficult family histories, we can extract important life skills.

There's no question that your parents' divorce affected your life. But it doesn't follow that you have to allow it to continue to do so. It's much like the old maxim, When life gives you lemons, make lemonade.

When you were a child your parents were powerful figures in your life. For example, when your parents embroiled you in their conflicts, you were too dependent and too frightened to stand up to them. As an adult, however, you do not need to be a pawn on their battlefield. You can refuse to allow them to continue to use and abuse you in that way. Kelly, who is now twenty-eight, just recently told her parents, "I would love to have you both here for Shana's [her daughter] first birthday party, but you may not spoil her day or mine by arguing. So, if you can't come and be pleasant with one another, then you are not invited." You may feel uncomfortable the first time you set some boundaries for what you are willing to tolerate, but after doing it a few times, you will likely feel very empowered.

You may not have the idyllic family you dreamed of or the family you thought other kids were lucky enough to have. That doesn't mean you can't make the most of the family that you do have. There are few absolutes in our lives and often the only thing within our control is how we *perceive* or *interpret* an event. For example, you can choose to see your family as rearranged or you can choose to see it as broken. If you choose the first, you are likely to have more positive feelings about your family. Instead of focusing on the damage, you can ask yourself, as we did the participants in this study, what strengths you gained from your parents' divorce, and then build on these. You can choose to go with the prevailing stereotypes or to challenge the societal messages about divorce that are likely steeped in myths rather than based on realities. In so doing, you may find yourself creating a new, more positive narrative about your family.

And finally, please, banish the label "adult child of divorce" from your vocabulary. Your parents divorced but that doesn't define who you are. It's a stigmatizing label that presumes you are deficient or traumatized or severely troubled because your parents divorced when you were a child. Of course, you may find that you have commonalities with other adults who grew up with divorced parents, but that's not enough of a reason to accept being glibly stereotyped. The next time someone applies that label to you, ask them to tell you what they think that says about you. And if you have fallen prey to using it to explain something about yourself, ask yourself if it is keeping you from making changes that might bring you more satisfaction in your life.

CONCLUSION

As we saw in the last chapter, the foundation of any family is designed by its architects: the parents. It is the parents' job to figure out the living arrangements and painstakingly develop their independent relationships with each of their children. As time moves on and feelings of loss subside, parents gradually begin a new chapter in their lives. Most merge with new partners, some gain more children in that process, and their families undergo another series of changes.

Helping our children face the challenges of living with family upheaval and the change that will follow means teaching them to be resilient, to cope with the reality of the changes in spite of the distress they may feel. It means supporting them emotionally, helping them build a strong foundation psychologically, *and* helping them find outside resources when they need them. It means facing the fact that for some kids changes will be a lot tougher to weather than for others, and it means helping those vulnerable ones develop the capacity to bounce back as best they can.

Chapter 9

ADVICE FROM
THE FRONT LINES

How to Script a Good Divorce

As we draw this book to a close it seems fitting to give the children the last word. With the wisdom of twenty years of experience apiece living in divorced families, the 173 adults we interviewed are experts at what does and doesn't matter *in the long run.*

At the end of our interviews, we posed two final questions:

- From your experience growing up in a divorced family, what advice would you give to parents who are divorcing?
- What advice would you give to other kids whose parents are divorcing?

Here's what the adult children had to say.

To Children:

TRY TO UNDERSTAND WHAT
YOUR PARENTS ARE GOING THROUGH.

Just remember your parents are in a lot of pain. You know it's not an easy decision to come to leave the person who you thought you'd be with for the rest of your life. And they're makin' it, like, on a whim. And you know, sometimes they just need to cry, and you just need to let 'em.

Remember that your parents' world is falling apart, too, just like yours is. That they're not always going to have their act together like parents should, 'cause they have so much stress going on.

IT'S NOT YOUR FAULT.

Don't blame yourself. If one of your parents is trying to pit you against your other parent, walk away.

It's not your fault. Sometimes when parents are getting divorced, people say mean things [that] they don't necessarily mean, whether it's about the opposing parent or even about you. Cling to whatever remains stable. If you've got friends don't be afraid to talk to them, because if they are good friends, they will be there to listen to it. And if they're not good friends, to hell with them. Don't take anything between your parents personally; don't let yourself get dragged into the middle of one of their fights, because it isn't your fault and it's only going to get rougher if you take it personally.

Know that it is not about your relationship with your parents, it is about the relationship with themselves.

AVOID BLAME GAMES.

Try not to take sides. The decision doesn't have anything to do with you.

Even though it may be difficult, don't let them use you, catch you in the middle.

Let people know what you want and need in the divorce settlement.

IT'S YOUR LIFE. DON'T USE THE DIVORCE
AS AN EXCUSE FOR NOT MOVING ON.

Don't use it as an excuse. You can succeed no matter what. Self-esteem doesn't come from others, but from yourself, and don't blame yourself.

The fact that your parents are getting a divorce is not an excuse to have bad behavior or let your future fall to the wayside.

You have to make a conscious effort as to where you want to go with your own life.

May have to step up the maturity level a little bit quicker and take more responsibility for yourself.

DEVELOP YOUR OWN IDENTITY.

Find some things that you want to do and get involved in them (for example, the swim team).

Hold strong to your own convictions and do what you need to do for yourself. Be strong in the decisions you make.

Get involved. Do things you really enjoy besides going to school and playing video games. Do things like soccer, or boys and girls clubs.

FIND SOMEONE TO WHOM YOU CAN TALK ABOUT IT— INCLUDING YOUR PARENTS.

Find someone to confide in: a peer, adult, whatever.

Don't be afraid to talk to your parents about what you're going through.

Talk to friends about it because there are a lot of other kids that are going through it, too.

Express your needs, desires and wants as early as possible. In time difficult feelings will heal. Be vocal about the logistics of what's happening in the divorce. Don't be afraid to express what you need.

Talk to people. Don't be afraid to say how you really feel and to talk, even if they don't want to hear it. Otherwise it stays in you and keeps eating at you.

Reach out to somebody—like a school counselor, friend's mother, someone who wouldn't judge you. Kids feel judged during a divorce. And, I would tell kids not to feel like they need to repress how they feel, not to hide their feelings. I did that a lot and it really makes it worse. I think things are different now—there are support groups for kids, and divorce is more common, but I still think these things are important.

Counseling, definitely, for both parents and kids, but kids separate; they need a chance to not have the parent there to talk. Ask as many questions as they need to ask. Talk to anybody that they feel they can talk to, maybe not always a parent either. Try not to hold anything in. If you feel like crying, you should cry.

Find a friend. I became so isolated, so I think that it would be some encouragement for kids, whatever age, to find somebody to be close to. And whether that's still one of the parents or an aunt or a teacher or a friend, that it's so easy to become very withdrawn. . . . Security, someone that you feel like will be there for you.

GOOD THINGS CAN HAPPEN. BE RESILIENT.

Try to have an open mind about it. Realize that it might be for your own good.

They're probably doing it for the best. They both love you. Just don't let it affect your life at all. Go on day by day.

Life can still be good. If both parents still love the kids, they can still have a good life. It doesn't have to be totally devastating. I don't believe people have to turn bad just because of a divorce.

It gets better and easier with time. Your parents still love you.

Try to give your love to both parents either way and real-ize that some of their decisions are [made in] your best interest. You're not loved any less because you're not with one parent or the other. In time things will get better. If you have hope, there's a way.

IT'S NOT THE END OF THE WORLD.

It's not the end of the world. Some people just can't live together anymore, and it would be harder for everybody if they stayed together.

Try to keep your chin up. . . . Get involved in activities. . . . talk to others about it and don't hold your anger inside. You can be happy and successful in your adult years. It is not the end of the world.

Parents deserve to have love, too. They deserve to be happy, too. Kids just need to accept that. They need to understand that in time it will be okay, and they need to find strength within themselves to do that. It may seem real tough at times but in the long run, [you] will eventu-ally see that [divorce is better] than being raised in a house where there is not love. But it all goes back to the parents to [help their kids] keep self-esteem, self-confidence, and self-worth, and to reassure the kids that it is not their fault. It has nothing to do with them.

To Parents:

If you are in the throes of divorce you can make the divorce less stressful by heeding the advice of these grown children. Their suggestions can help you navigate the difficult road ahead. If you have been divorced for a while you may be wishing you could turn back the clock and do things differently regarding your separation and divorce, not to mention your marriage. As parents, we all carry feelings about difficult times in our lives when we wish we could have acted differently, even if only for the sake of our children. Although we can't, of course, go back and undo the errors of our past, the thoughts and reflections of the adult children quoted throughout this book and below should be evidence enough that it is never too late to make changes and improve your family situation. Here's what the kids had to say.

DON'T PUT THE KIDS IN THE MIDDLE.

Don't put kids in the middle; don't make kids the jury; don't make visitation difficult; don't speak ill of the other parent. Kids don't care whose fault it is. Don't blame each other. Each of you is responsible.

Don't put your kids in the middle. That's the biggest thing. I think that the anger that they feel between each other shouldn't be put on the kids, that they should always keep the kids in mind. This is the biggest thing that you've got to do, especially if you've got little kids. Just leave the kids out of it, totally.

Keep your differences away from the kids so they don't have to listen to it, and don't make them make choices or choose between each other and don't screw with the kids' minds.

Keep your differences private. Don't let the kids hear it and don't make the kids feel guilty. Don't make one be the messenger for the other.

Do whatever it takes to parent well together— and don't bad-mouth each other.

No matter what the cost to you, no matter how much it hurts, it is so important that you not bad-mouth the other parent in front of the kids. Please, be civil in front of your kids.

You don't have to be best friends, but don't play the little games that people who are divorcing tend to play. Be fair. Try not to make it an ugly divorce. Try to at least remain civil in front of the kids.

Get over yourself enough to quit being so selfish. Any two people can get along if they're selfless enough.

Watch out what you're doing in front of your children. And also, be careful how you treat one another, you know, say hi, good night, good morning, good-bye, etc. So many parents are lacking in those basic getting-along skills!

Watch how you behave in front of the kids—don't use them as tools for revenge, be mindful of children and when discussing custody, never bad-mouth the exspouse; he/she's still your child's parent.

Get rid of your hostility, or mask it if you can't. Don't cut your spouse down. Don't attack the other parent's treat-ment of the children. Also don't talk poorly about your

exspouse in front of your children, no matter if it kills
you. Your children lose a lot of respect for you if you do
that.

If you can't remain friends, [you] need to remain civil and
concentrate on what's best for your kids, which my parents did, rather than on what's best for you.

Put yourself in your kids' shoes. For your children's sake,
bite your tongue, don't say anything bad about the other
parent. Keep the problems away from the children.

I think it's important not to say things about the other
spouse in front of the children. As a child, I really looked
up to both my parents, and when one of them would say
something bad about the other, it would put me in the
position of agreeing and thinking something bad about the
other parent, or disagreeing and putting me in conflict
with the parent. That's hard for parents to do, but I think
it's really important.

Keep a good relationship going for the kids. And no matter how you feel about your ex, when you're in front of
the children, *don't* let it show.

PUT YOUR CHILDREN FIRST.

If at all possible, think of the children first. Children are
not a weapon. Try and take a deep breath and, if at all possible, come to a reasonable solution; try and be reasonable.

Think about what's best for the child, not what is best for
you.

Try your best to work things out. Communicate, and don't expose the kids to disagreements and conflict. Parents don't understand how children are affected.

Put feelings aside so that your kids can have a childhood. Remember that the kids are first. In the long run, they'll remember whether or not you kept that in mind.

Remember your kids and that you came together once for something and you can come together again for the same things. You may have your differences but you have a similarity, the kids.

Get along. Worry about the kids, not who gets what money or who gets the couch. And go to family therapy!

STAY INVOLVED IN YOUR KIDS' LIVES.

There's no reason to pretend that everything is the same as it was when everything is obviously different. But if you make an effort, you can maintain a relationship with your children that's strong, even though you (and they) are going through all these changes.

Set up a good custody schedule so you can both see your kids a lot and never make kids pick favorites.

Make sure that you call your kids. Call your kids and be a humongous part of their life.

Just because you do not live in the same house does not mean that you do not need to have equal responsibility.

TALK TO YOUR KIDS.

Get your kids more involved, let them know what's going on. Talk to them, be open with them.

Communication is the key. Always talk to your kids as far as what's going on and what's happening. If things seem scary, still tell them how it is; don't sugarcoat it at all.

Be as candid as you can with your kids given their age level. Keep the conflict you have with your soon-to-be-ex away from them as much as possible. They're obviously affected by it, but they shouldn't be in the middle of it.

Explain to your kids why [you're divorcing]. Make sure that they know that you love them and that it's not their fault. I never had the "It's my fault" issue—but I had a lot of friends who thought [their parents' divorce] was their fault and that's an ugly thing to see in, like, you know, a ten-year-old kid. But, uh, yeah, make sure they understand why and don't lie to them, for God's sake. I hate that, when you hear about parents lying to their kids about why they're getting a divorce.

REASSURE THEM OFTEN: IT'S NOT THEIR FAULT.

Be sure your kids know that the issues at hand are your problem and have nothing to do with them. I don't think you can say that enough times to a child.

Keep using the love word as much as possible, because I think that when some kids go through divorce they do think it's them.

Try to live nearby.

Proximity of the two residences was very important in our case.

Stay involved in your kids' lives. Don't move across the country.

Kids need to stay in one place. Moving from place to place to place, changing schools, having to make new friends all the time is really difficult for children. Because I went back and forth for a while there before going out on my own I know you need the stability.

Friends of my mother's separated and they rented an apartment and took turns living in the house with the kids or in the apartment. So the kids always stayed in the house and the parents did the flip-flopping. When I heard that, I thought it was the most wonderful thing anyone had done for kids of divorce. I know that that's not an option for a lot of families, or if there's abuse or if the couple absolutely cannot get along. . . . But that couple put their children's well-being first. I respect them so much for that.

Get the plans straight.

Try to work things out so kids aren't distressed over who they will be with, and when they will be with each parent.

I also think that having a really sound structure to what the divorce means to the family afterward in terms of the exact dates and times that you'll be with Mom and be with Dad and what you will be doing and when you'll see your brothers and have all of that so you know when to expect it and you can feel comfortable knowing that that discipline will still be there and that will be your new family.

AND WHATEVER YOU DO, DON'T STAY TOGETHER FOR THE SAKE OF THE CHILDREN.

Don't stay together just for the children, because they're smart. They can feel the tension; they can feel what's going on around them. And that could be more detrimental to them than the parent leaving.

If parents aren't happy and the kids are young don't try to keep the relationship together just for the kids and then realize ten years down the line that it still never has worked out. I just think that staying together just for the kids' sake isn't necessarily the best thing.

Don't wait too long and don't use the kids as an excuse for staying together. That is why my parents did stay together. All it does is put a big burden on the kids, saying they are the glue that is holding them together. Try hard to keep it together, but not because you have kids. Just cut the apron strings; the kids do not need that.

I'm very lucky that my parents divorced when I was really young, 'cause I don't remember a lot of it. And in a way I feel that's good, because I don't have any bad memories of [the divorce]."

At the time it might all seem negative, but as I look back I think there were a lot of positive things that happened in my life because of the divorce. Not because they didn't get divorced.

Don't sacrifice your happiness for your children . . . and just love yourself, because if you don't, your children are certainly not going to love you.

Try to stay together as best as you can. Try to work it out. If it's worse for the kids that you stay together, then you should get a divorce. Always keep a positive role in your kids' lives.

Get over it and move on! Life is short.

IN CONCLUSION

As you can see, what seems to matter most to kids over the years is the most basic stuff: They want you to get along with your ex, to not put them in the middle, to be consistent, to communicate. They want you to be straight with them; they want you to be happy; and they want you to act like grown-ups. You don't have to like your ex, you don't even have to be amicable, but, for the sake of your children, you *do* need to learn to be civil with one another. There's just no getting around it, and the reason is quite simple and bears repeating: The persistence of interparental conflict has negative consequences for children.

If you divorce without children you can part and not speak with one another ever again. But, as a responsible parent, when you have children it's not possible to terminate your parenting relationship without causing them harm. Your children will provide you with many opportunities to improve your relationship with your ex. Try looking at them as ways of helping your children build their sense of family. That's what children want after all. When the rubber hits the road, most kids would rather have a large tribe they can call family than two parents living together without love. And being civil with your ex is perhaps the largest contribution you can make to that family feeling, and you just might find that it makes your life feel more whole, too.

Learning to act as civilized adults, bound together by parenting, is not as difficult as it may feel at first. It means you need to think before you speak and practice being as polite as you would be with most other people in your life. Most divorced couples struggle with residual anger, but remember this: Hanging on to anger has no advantages. All it does is upset your children and hamper your opportunities to improve your life. Take a good look at what's holding you back from letting it go and moving on. It's not that you don't have good cause, it's just that it serves no good purpose and hurts both you and your children.

As you look at your anger don't overlook how your unrealistic expectations may be fueling it. Many angry exspouses, even years after their divorce, keep refueling their anger each time their ex does something they don't like. Ask yourself whether his or her behavior surprises you. Most likely it doesn't. Most likely you'll say that it's typical of something he or she *always* did in the past. Then ask yourself why you expect him or her to change. Most likely you'll discover that you spent years trying to change that behavior when you were married, and you failed. So, why would you expect him or her to change now?

If you must, tell yourself that there is absolutely nothing to gain and everything to lose in freely expressing your anger. Put on your saint's cap and if your ex says something that makes you angry, don't respond directly, but move on to a safer playing field. There are many situations in life that call on us to act civilized when we don't feel like it. You know how to do it.

Not expressing your anger doesn't mean that you have to forgive your ex. While forgiving would be an added bonus, not expressing anger just means accepting the reality of what *is* and accepting your ex as your child's parent. If you still find yourself consumed by your anger, get some help. It's never too late. Counseling, support groups and friends can be helpful in uncovering the hidden traps that are preventing you from moving on.

When your children acquire new relatives, as they most likely will, it's important that you acknowledge these people and respect the new relationships. It can be upsetting when your ex has a new baby and your daughter excitedly tells you every detail about her new brother. As she proudly shows you the picture of her holding the new baby you may feel pangs of jealousy, or perhaps you'll feel left out or even threatened that your child will want to spend more time with your ex and her new family. Although these are normal feelings, you want to be careful about sharing them with your child. You don't have to go overboard to share in the excitement but you do need to let your child know that it's okay to talk about his new sibling in your home. Otherwise your child will learn that he has to keep his "other" family a secret from you. Keeping secrets from one parent about their life in the other parent's household makes children feel divided between them.

To help your child feel comfortable with her binuclear family you have to respect her new kinship bonds. Doing so not only helps your child but it will help you feel more a part of your child's life. You may even be surprised that, as the years pass, these relationships begin to feel like family to you, too.

Many divorced people feel very strange around their former in-laws. You may not know quite the right term to attach to these folks who once were family, especially if your ex's sister's daughter who you last saw when she was twelve still calls you "aunt" even though she's now twenty-two. As the years go by, however, you may find some comfort in seeing them again. Greeting a former sister-in-law who was once a close friend, or a niece with whom you were close years ago, helps us feel more connected to our past. Maybe they won't feel quite like family anymore, but you may be surprised at how good it feels to integrate the past with the present. Isn't that why we go to school and family reunions? Seeing your ex's family again may, indeed, bring back a host of warm memories and remind you that you all, still, belong to the same family tribe.

After divorce, families expand vertically as well as horizontally. New members join through cohabitation and marriage, and new births bring forth the next generation. As they share the circles of life through weddings, births and deaths, how they are related becomes far less important than the personal connections they develop.

My younger daughter's wedding is coming up in a few months and once again we will have the occasion to celebrate together. We'll be three generations of "exes, steps, halves and fulls" blending together as one family. We're getting accustomed to being together now and I look forward to these life events as opportunities to share our lives and create family memories. Like all types of families, these occasions are important markers that strengthen our bonds. Having more than the usual amount of parents may confuse onlookers, but the medium will clearly deliver the message: *We are family.*

Postscript

A CALL FOR CHANGE

How Society Can Support Families after Divorce

I guess the only way to stop divorce is to stop marriage.

WILL ROGERS

The story of how divorce affects children over the long term is not complete without looking at the societal factors that impinge on a family's well-being. In the United States the more than 18 million children who live with divorced parents do not receive the same social, political and financial supports as do children in married families. In the current social climate, married families are rewarded, while those families that deviate from this "one household, two married parents" model are punished. Children with divorced parents are viewed as deficient because they lack two biological parents who reside in one household. This reinforces negative images instead of providing positive messages and models that would help children's self-esteem.

I don't want to imply that there haven't been positive changes in divorce-related policies and legislation over the past three decades. The introduction of no-fault divorce, for example, was a monumental step forward. Its intent, to make divorce less punitive, indicated an important shift in our view of divorce by acknowledging that divorcing adults have the right to terminate their marriage in a court of law without having to defend their reasons or assign fault to their spouse. Further progress was made when joint custody legislation emerged, introducing the controversial view that, even after divorce, both parents are still guardians of their children's welfare.

Although neither no-fault nor joint custody legislation has completely achieved its objectives, over the past decade the progress toward serving the best interests of children is noteworthy. The adversarial process continues to operate despite no-fault legislation, but newer models aimed at reducing conflict between parents are gaining acceptance. As more divorcing couples seek to divorce with less acrimony, alternative options, such as mediation and collaborative law, are growing in popularity. Some jurisdictions now even mandate mediation, relying on judicial hearings only in those cases when mediation fails to resolve the dispute. Court-affiliated divorce services have responded to these changes by replacing their long-standing reconciliation counseling services with educational and early intervention programs geared to help parents learn how to cooperate more effectively. Equally important is the fact that divorced parents and their children experience less stigma than their counterparts did three decades ago, not solely related to these legislative changes but because of the sheer increase in the numbers of divorced parents and their children. Another important mark of our progress is the increasing proliferation of research that addresses a more balanced understanding of divorce and its effects on children.

Why, then, with these important changes, am I waving the red flag of concern? Because we are experiencing a powerful backlash that threatens to obliterate the important social changes achieved during the past three decades. Causing a powerful wave of panic across this nation is the fact that dramatic changes in contemporary family life make the Norman Rockwell images of family life obsolete.

In a nutshell, marriage is no longer the foundation of the family. When added to the more than one million families each year who experience divorce, the dramatic increase and social acceptance of cohabitation and single parenting means that millions of children are growing up in families with unmarried parents. According to the Census Bureau, only 25 percent of households today fit the "one household, two married parents" model and by 2010 it is projected to drop to 20 percent. This unprecedented demographic shift has led many to view divorce as a plague on the family landscape, a threat to the very foundations of our society.

In reaction, a powerful movement is afoot to bring marriage back as the mainstay of American family life by rewarding married families and punishing unmarried parents. Funds from the federal government are flowing into programs to encourage and support marriage, such as paying welfare mothers who marry the fathers of their children, irrespective of the quality of their relationship.

One way the "marriage-savers" hope to overturn the tides of social change is by calling for more restrictive and punitive divorce laws. By making divorce more difficult, they conclude that fewer people will divorce, thereby providing healthier environments for children. What they neglect to take into account is that by forcing parents to stay in bad marriages they may actually make it worse for children by escalating interparental conflict. They also want the courts to reintroduce reconciliation counseling programs (despite their lack of effectiveness) at the expense of cutting back on newer programs that help divorcing parents cooperate more effectively.

The continued demonizing of divorce as the culprit of family breakdown has been a deterrent to changes that would support families challenged by marital uncoupling. When we cling to the past as an ideal for the future, we need to preserve that picture by slaying the dragons that we perceive as threatening. Divorce heads the list of these "threatening dragons" and increasingly, as negative myths are challenged, much blood is shed.

I am certainly in favor of strengthening marriages but I want us to do that without punishing those who are not married, either by choice or by the lack of opportunity. Although some children who live in one-parent households are at a disadvantage and may exhibit more behavioral problems than their two-parent family counterparts, we cannot conclude that marriage itself is the determining factor in the well-being of our children. The research very clearly shows that children thrive in families where there are loving, nurturing adults to guide and care for them and adequate environments to meet their basic health and safety needs, irrespective of legal marital ties. Troubles tend to arise in those families where children are not provided with these critical resources. Most single-parent households are headed by women and, on average, women still earn considerably less than their male counterparts. Although it can easily *appear* as if divorce itself is burdening children, when we take a closer look we see that the issue is not simply the structure of the family per se. It is the lack of sufficient resources. In fact, a recent study in the *Journal of the American Medical Association* found that when the income of poverty-level families improved, children's behavioral symptoms were reduced by 40 percent.

Many European countries have stronger safety nets for children, even in those countries where there are higher rates of cohabitation and lower rates of marriage than in the United States. They have longer subsidized maternity leave policies, better part-time work for mothers, more comprehensive health care, and more government-funded child-care opportunities. These policies affect *all* children, not merely those who live with married parents. In contrast to our policies that attempt to influence and shape choices people make about their family relationships, these policies support the diversity of family forms that people are choosing to live in. Our lack of these family-friendly policies puts poor families at a serious disadvantage. Even if a single-parent mother can find paid work, she is unlikely, without governmental support, to earn enough money to meet her children's health- and child-care needs.

We cannot afford to waste our valuable resources in a "culture war" aimed at fighting change. If we are really concerned about the emotional and physical health of our children, we need to respond to our children's current realities and not to the way we might wish things to be. We need to move beyond our outdated infrastructure and make governmental resources available to all parents. Parenting and family are no longer dependent on marriage, and the time has come for us to stop holding up the nuclear family as the paragon of moral righteousness and instead embrace and respect our diverse family forms and kinship ties.

Efforts to reduce divorce rates by prolonged waiting periods and fault-based divorce laws only serve to prolong parental conflicts and increase their financial costs, thereby being detrimental to children. Rather than spending our valuable resources in such misguided efforts we need to encourage more humane divorce that minimizes emotional pain and financial distress to families. We can accomplish this by demanding that our legal system support the speedy and inexpensive resolution of marital disputes. We must challenge the negative message that divorcing spouses are necessarily adversaries and recast our thinking to reinforce responsible parenting and family continuity after divorce. The judicial use of mediation, collaborative law and other conflict-reducing methods can help parents resolve their disputes more quickly, thereby having the potential to result in less acrimony and a reduction in economic costs to the family. We need to recognize that gender and parenting roles are in a state of flux, and this is reflected in children's living arrangements after divorce, which make these roles less clear-cut than they once were. The ideals of joint custody emerged precisely because of the changes in gender roles and, just like many married parents, divorced parents are struggling with new ways to parent effectively and have well-functioning families. Deciding on the best workable living arrangements for our children requires knowledge and flexibility. Educational and early intervention programs offer support and direction to divorcing parents and their children by providing healthy models, teaching problem-solving and conflict-reducing skills.

With nearly half of American marriages ending in divorce, the best thing we can do for our children is turn our attention toward helping their parents improve their chances for having a *good* divorce. In the end, what is in the best interest of the children is ensuring that they live in healthy families, regardless of their parents' marital status.

APPENDIX:

The Research

The findings in this book were based on the results of the Binuclear Family Study, a two-decade longitudinal investigation that followed the lives of divorced families for over twenty years. The study began in 1979 with intensive interviews with ninety-eight pairs of exspouses, all of whom had minor children. Interviews were conducted at three points in time (one, three, and five years after the legal divorce) and new partners (stepparents and cohabiting partners) were interviewed twice over the five years (see Ahrons, 1981, 1984; Ahrons, 1998; Ahrons & Miller, 1993; Ahrons & Rodgers, 1987; Ahrons & Wallisch, 1987, Ahrons & Wallisch, 1987). The subjects were randomly selected from the public divorce records in Dane County, Wisconsin, and included twenty-eight families with joint custody, fifty-four families with mother custody, and sixteen families with father custody. The response rate at five years was 90 percent. The initial funds for the study were provided by NIMH and the University of Wisconsin.

These findings are based primarily on the fourth wave of

interviews, conducted in 1999/2000, a little over twenty years since the first interview. The funds for this stage of the study were provided by the State of California Center for Families and Children, the Foundation for the Contemporary Family, the University of Southern California, and the Radcliffe Institute for Advanced Study at Harvard. The major focus was to examine adult children's perceptions of their parents' divorces twenty years afterward. The Binuclear Family Study is particularly significant in its ability to simultaneously look at divorce and remarriage within the same family over time. It allows us to compare the parents' perspectives during the first six years following the divorce with their children's perspectives twenty years later. It is unique in several ways: (1) it is the only twenty-year longitudinal investigation drawn from a random, nonclinical sample; (2) it has the ability to compare the long-term effects on children of different custody arrangements; (3) it is one of few studies to draw upon data collected from both parents and stepparents in the early formative postdivorce years; (4) it is the only study that specifically compares parents' and adult children's perceptions of the divorced parents' coparenting style; and (5) rather than focusing on a target child, as most studies do, this study benefits from its ability to compare siblings' perspectives.

DATA COLLECTION

The children, who were all over the age of eighteen, were located through a variety of means. When we could not find them through computer search engines and online telephone books, we contacted one or both of their parents and requested their children's phone numbers and addresses. Our male subjects were more easily found because their names remained the same, whereas for our female subjects who had remarried we had to depend more on finding their whereabouts through either their siblings or their parents.

This yielded an eligible and locatable sample of 193 from the total population of 204 adult children. Of those 11 individuals who were not considered part of the original sample, 1 was ineligible because her parents had remarried one another, several other children were disabled, 2 had died, and the few remaining ones were unlocatable. From the 193 who were locatable, we completed interviews with 173, an unusually high response rate of 90 percent. These 173 adult children represented 89 of the original 98 families.

While the parents were interviewed in person in Waves 1–3, the interviews with the adult children were all conducted over the telephone. Research has indicated that telephone interviews are a reliable and valid methodological approach. One of the strengths of this study is that these were not "cold" interviews. We have a wealth of information about our subjects' families over a five-year period earlier in their lives. From the parent interviews, extensive genograms about subjects' families were available. The ability to talk about members of the participants' families by name piqued their interest and allowed the interviewers to establish rapport quickly with participants. Doctoral students with clinical experience conducted the interviews. All the interviews were tape-recorded and then transcribed.

The interviews were semistructured, prompting for both quantitative and qualitative responses. Consistent with qualitative methodology, during these portions of the interview, participants were encouraged to tell their stories in their own words with as much elaboration as they wished; interviewers probed where indicated. The interview schedule was organized to gather information about family processes over time—from the years preceding the divorce to the present—with particular attention paid to the time of parental divorce and (if relevant) subsequent remarriages. Interviews lasted between one and two hours, focusing on the ways in which parental divorce altered, expanded, damaged, and/or strengthened family relationships over time. When indicated, either because of lack of time to complete the interview or because it would be beneficial to get more information from the subject, a second interview was scheduled.

Recent research has found that children's retrospective reports are quite stable and that such reports are reasonably accurate. Our interest was in how the adult children perceived and attached meaning to the events surrounding parental divorce, rather than whether or not such perceptions represented some absolute truth. The Principal Investigator holds strongly to the view that "objective fact" is, in reality, colored by perception— one's perceptions of an event or a process govern one's feelings and behavior. For example, two children who experienced the same event often perceive it quite differently and, over the course of their lives, form different attitudes based on these perceptions. Our intent was not to identify a consistent set of objective facts about the participants' parents' divorces, but rather to identify the consequences of the divorce as experienced by the grown children and to understand the process by which he or she came to this experience. We wanted to hear the voices of adult children as they reflected upon the effects of their parents' divorces twenty years ago.

SAMPLE

The parent sample was predominantly white and middle class. At the first interview, the majority of the parents were in their mid-thirties. Their marriages had lasted, on average, ten years, and the families averaged two children (range was one to five). At the time of the divorce, 20% of the children were preschool age, 50% were elementary school age, and 30% were adolescents. Seventy-five percent (75%) of the mothers were employed, and a little over half of the fathers and 38% of the mothers had college degrees.

At the time of their interviews, the grown children (eighty-four women and eighty-nine men) ranged in age from 21 to 52 (M = 31.31, SD = 6.31). Although the initial criterion for parent participation was that the parents had a minor child, all adult children in the family were interviewed, so ten participants were over 18 at the time of the divorce. Most of the adult children were well-educated: 23% had completed postgraduate training or professional school, 33% had completed college, 31% had completed some postsecondary training, 10% had received their high school diplomas, and 3% had completed their education before receiving their high school diplomas.

The majority (85%) of these adult children were employed; 32% were professional, technical or kindred workers. Fifty-two percent (n = 90) of them reported being either currently or previously married: 29% (n = 26) had divorced, and of those 26, 17 remained unmarried. At the time of the study, 42% were married. Of those 58% who reported being unmarried, slightly over half said that they were in a serious relationship, and half of these said they were cohabiting. Of the 68 who were parents, almost all of them (n = 63) had at least 1 biological child; 5 reported having adopted or stepchildren. The mean age marking their transition to parenthood was 27 (range was 18–37). In terms of their ages when parents were divorced, 27% were between 1 and 5, 34% were between 5 and 10, 29% were between 11 and 17, and 5% were over 21 years of age.

The families that most of these adult children grew up in are now very complex. Seventy-one percent (71%) of their mothers remarried, as did 86% of their fathers (figures are consistent with national statistics). Of those mothers and fathers who did remarry, 10% and 12% experienced a second divorce, respectively. Of the 89 binuclear families represented by the 173 adult children, 64% experienced the remarriage of both parents, and all but 8% of children gained stepsiblings, half siblings, or both. Note that in only 5% of the families, had neither parent remarried.

Of the 173 adult children in this sample, 14% of the children were only children ($n = 24$) and thus did not have any full siblings. The majority of the adult children in the sample had 1 sibling (46%; $n = 80$). Twenty of the adult children had 2 siblings (12%), 35 of the adult children had 3 siblings (20%), 6 of the adult children had 5 siblings (4%) and 8 of the adult children had 8 siblings (5%).

MEASURES AND CONSTRUCTS

The primary independent variable was the divorced coparenting relationship, as perceived by both parents and their children. In analyses from the parents' interviews in earlier phases of the Binuclear Family Study, a factor analysis of 13 individual items was employed to develop a typology of coparenting styles, ranging from cooperative and supportive to highly conflicted and destructive. For each couple, an average of "his" and "her" scores was used to form a couple score. For the Wave 4 interviews with the children we described each of the five coparenting typologies and asked the subjects to tell us which categories best described their parents' relationship with one another at two periods of time: (1) shortly after the divorce; and (2) at the present time. The children's retrospective and current perceptions of their parents' coparental relationship quality are correlated with all three reports of the parents' account of their relationship (children's and parents' reports of coparental relationship quality are correlated between .20 and .59; $p < .01$ for all correlations).

The primary dependent variables are comprised of four major constructs: (1) quality of each parent-child relationship; (2) degree of presence or absence of loyalty conflicts; (3) binuclear family cohesion; and (4) self-assessments of the long-term effects of their parents' divorce. In addition, a major focus of interest was to identify differences between siblings.

ANALYTIC TECHNIQUES

A wide variety of analytic techniques were used to assess differences in the average level of family functioning and to identify different types of families. Cluster analysis was used to identify the types of relationships between divorced parents and how they changed over time. For example, the groups in chapter 7 were identified in this way. Composite variables of different constructs were made by combining information from various informants and measures.

In the first stage of data analysis the reliability and factor structure of measures representing each of the central constructs were established. When the psychometric properties of the scaled items were established (alpha coefficients above .7 and single factor solutions with factor loadings over .6), additive scale scores were constructed to operationalize each construct.

The research questions asked how past and current coparenting relationships affect the current quality of the parent-child relationship. Previous research by the principal investigator had established that five types of coparenting adequately classify the major coparenting styles in divorced families (Ahrons, 1987). Therefore, these types formed the basis for additional analyses. Three versions of coparenting types were assessed: current coparenting as perceived by the adult child, coparenting twenty years ago as recollected by the adult child, and coparenting as reported by parents twenty years ago.

Since each of the representations of coparenting was measured categorically, analysis of variance (ANOVA) was used to inspect mean differences in each of the three study outcomes across types of coparenting. Post hoc tests (e.g., Scheffe, Tukey) were used to assess pairwise differences in intergenerational outcomes between types in order to account for Type II error associated with multiple comparisons. Social and demographic characteristics of children (i.e., marital status, age, gender, income, number of siblings) were adjusted as covariates in the models. If correspondence among the coparenting classification schemes were not excessive, two- and three-way ANOVAs were also performed to examine how the three schemes uniquely influenced current intergenerational outcomes. In addition, *transitions* in the coparenting relationship over twenty years, as reported by each adult child, were used to construct variables reflecting the most common changes in coparenting types. Transition variables were used in multiple regression analyses to predict the three intergenerational outcomes.

More detailed information on methods and data analyses are presented in the selected references. Numerous student papers, master's theses and doctoral dissertations were also completed based on the data from the study. The data from the first 3 waves of interviews are archived at the Murray Research Center at Harvard and can be accessed by request for academic analyses. Wave 4 data will be archived in 2005.

NOTES

INTRODUCTION

xiii *"life, marriage, and the family"* Judith S. Wallerstein and Joan Berlin Kelly. *Surviving the Breakup* (New York: Basic Books, 1980), p. 328.

CHAPTER 1:
NO EASY ANSWERS

7 *". . . new institutions and values"* Stephanie Coontz, *The Way We Never Were* (New York: Basic Books, 1992), p. 230.

12 *less than 25 percent of all households* Jason Fields and Lynne Casper (2001) America's Families and Living Arrangements: March 3000. Current Population Reports, p. 20–537. Washington, D.C.: U.S. Census Bureau

15 *children's needs but how* See the following articles for more information: Constance Ahrons, "Redefining the Divorced Family: A Conceptual Framework for Postdivorce Family System Reorganization," *Social Work* 25 (1980), 437–41; "Divorce: A Crisis of Family Transition and Change," *Family Relations* 29 (1980) 533-40; "Joint Custody Arrangements in the Postdivorce Family," *Journal of Divorce* 3 (1980) 189-205; and "The Binuclear Family: Two Households, One Family," *Alternative Lifestyles* (1979) 499–515.

19 *parents and their children* Judith Wallerstein and Sandra Blakeslee, "Children After Divorce," *New York Times* (January 22, 1989), p. 19.

19 *interviewed in this age group* Judith Wallerstein and Sandra Blakeslee, *Second Chances* (New York: Ticknor & Fields, 1989), Table 2 appendix, p. 315.

21   *hope for them to live* Rebecca Gardyn, Unmarried Bliss, *American Demographics* (December 2000) 22 , p. 61.

CHAPTER 2:
THE ADULT CHILDREN SPEAK

29   *are employed as professionals* Most of the adult children were well educated: thirty-nine (*n* = 39; 23%) completed a postgraduate training program or professional school; fifty-seven (*n* = 57; 33%) completed college; fifty-four (*n* = 54; 31%) completed some postsecondary training; eighteen (18; 10.4%) received their high school diplomas; and five (*n* = 5; 3%) completed their education before they received their high school diplomas. There were no differences in the highest level of education completed by men and women in this sample. Moreover, there were no significant differences between highest level of education completed and age at the time that, at the time of assessment, even the adult children who were the youngest at the time of their parents' divorce had achieved commensurate levels of educational attainment as the adult children who were older at the time of their parents' divorce.

At the time of the wave 4 interviews, the majority of adult children in this sample were employed (*n* = 147; 85%). Adult children most often reported that they were "professionals and technical or kindred workers (e.g., artists, writers)" (*n* = 55; 32%); "managers and administrators" (*n* = 27; 16%); and "craftsmen, foremen, and kindred workers (e.g., enlisted officer)" (*n* = 18; 10%). The remaining adult children reported that they were employed as "sales workers and service workers," and eleven (*n* = 11; 6%) reported that they were "full-time students."

29   *late adolescence or young adulthood*
AGE GROUP AT TIME OF DIVORCE TABLE

Age Group	Number of Children	Percentage of Children
0–4 Preschool	35	20 %
5–10 Middle Childhood	69	40 %
11–15 Early Adolescence	45	26 %

16–20 Late Adolescence	16	9 %
21+ Young Adulthood	8	5 %

Total n = 173

29   *who have married have divorced* E. Mavis Hetherington and John Kelly, *For Better or For Worse* (New York: W.W. Norton and Co., 2002).That half of the subjects were married is consistent with Hetherington's sample in which 40% had married and Wallerstein's sample in which 60% of her subjects had married. The 29% divorce rate fits in with the national norms. A report from the Department of Health and Human Services, Vital and Health Statistics, Series 23, Number 22, July 2002, shows that after ten years, 32% of white women's marriages have ended in divorce.

For first marriages ending in divorce among women aged twenty-five to twenty-nine, the median length of marriage before divorce in 1990 was 3.4 years (U.S. Bureau of the Census, 1992, p. 4).

29   *lived with their partners*

ADULT CHILDREN'S CURRENT
(AT TIME OF INTERVIEW) RELATIONSHIPS IN BRIEF:

Relationship Status	*Number of Adult Children*	*Percentage of Adult Children*
Married, first and only time	62	36%
Divorced and Remarried	11	6%
Not married; not involved in a significant relationship	46	27%
Not married; involved in a noncohabiting significant relationship	27	16%
Not married; involved in a cohabiting, significant relationship	27	16%

Total n = 173

Seventeen of the adult children were divorced and had not remarried. Thirteen reported that they had divorced one partner; three previously divorced two partners; one adult child reported that she had experienced the death of her spouse.

30   *or their father's remarriages*

FAMILY ORGANIZATIONAL CHART

89 Families
• Neither Parent Remarried: 4 (4.5%)
• Only Mother Remarried: 8 (9%)
  • Neither Step or Half: 3
  • Step Only: 3
  • Half Only: 2
  • Both Step and Half: 0
• Only Mother Remarried: 8 (9%)
  • Neither Step or Half: 3
  • Step Only: 3
  • Half Only: 2
  • Both Step and Half: 0
• Only Father Remarried: 21 (23.6%)
  • Neither Step or Half: 6
  • Step Only: 11
  • Half Only: 2
  • Both Step and Half: 2
• Both Remarried: 56 (62.9%)
  • Neither Step or Half: 7
  • Step Only: 22
  • Half Only: 11
  • Both Step and Half: 16

32   *self-blame and judgment* Dulwich Center (www.dulwichcentre .com) Externalising—Commonly Asked Questions.

34   *over the recent past* In the period between 1992 and 1994, 76% of respondents in the National Survey of Families and Households (NSFH) believed that "marriage is a lifetime relationship and should never be ended except under extreme circumstances" (Center for Demography and Ecology, University of Wisconsin, 1997). Furthermore, research continues

to show that most Americans view marriage as a central and defining institution in their lives, and that, in fact, its importance may be increasing.

34   *terminated without stigma* See Margaret Mead, "Anomalies in American Postdivorce Relationships," in Paul Bohannan, ed. *Divorce and After* (New York: Doubleday and Company, 1970).

38   *relationships and marriage* Valarie King, "Parental divorce and interpersonal trust in adult offspring," *Journal of Marriage and Family* 64 (August 2002) pp. 642–56.

CHAPTER 3:
LINGERING MEMORIES ABOUT
THEIR PREDIVORCE FAMILY

48   *rooted in their parents' marriage* In a study of several thousand British who were followed from birth to age thirty-three, the researchers found that " children whose parents would later divorce already showed more emotional problems at age seven than children from families that would remain together. The gap widened as the divorces occurred and the children reached adulthood, suggesting that divorce did have a detrimental long-term effect on some of them. But a large share of the gap preceded the divorces and might have appeared even had the parents stayed together." A. J. Cherlin, P. L. Chase-Lansdale, and C. McRae, "Effects of Parental Divorce on Mental Health Throughout the Life Course," *American Sociological Review* 63 (1998) 239–49; P. K. Kiernan, P .K. Robins, D. R. Morrison, and J. 0. Teitler, "Longitudinal Studies of Effects of Divorce on Children in Great Britain and the United States," *Science* 252 (June 7, 1991): 1386-89; P. L. Chase-Lansdale, A. J. Cherlin, and K.E. Kiernan, "The Long-Term Effects of Parental Divorce on the Mental Health of Young Adults: A Developmental Perspective," *Child Development* 66 (1995) 1614–34; A. J. Cherlin, "Going to extremes: Family structure, children's well-being, and social science," *Demography* (November 1999); and Carol L. Gohm, Shigehiro Oishi, Janet Darlington, and Ed Diener, "Culture, Parental Conflict, Parental Marital Status, and the Subjective Well-Being of Young Adults," *Journal of Marriage and the Family* (May 1998).

52   *devitalized, or high conflict* Almost one-third of the adult children described their parents' marriages as devitalized or good enough. Another

third described their parents' marriages as high-conflict, with frightening fights and prolonged hostilities that often lasted years. The final third of the children were under seven and had few if any memories of the predivorce family at all.

59 *predate the marriage* Almost all of the violent marriages included alcohol or other substance abuse, though not all parents who abused alcohol were violent. Of the more than 25% of children who said their parents abused alcohol (most of them in high-conflict marriages), their fathers were three times more likely to have the alcohol problem than their mothers. These parents' interviews several years after the divorce revealed that, in addition to alcohol abuse and violence, parents were more depressed, anxious and had other deep-seated psychological problems than parents did in the other two groups. It is highly likely that most of these parents had psychological problems prior to their marriages and these problems then dominated and defined the marriage.

59 *common in high-conflict marriages* More than 20% of the adult children we interviewed remembered physical violence between their parents. Of these, half described the violence as frequent and ongoing. Half of the children in this group were themselves physically abused, usually by their father.

CHAPTER 4:
LIVING ARRANGEMENTS

71 *any standardized list* For an excellent discussion of the determination of custody, see Joan B. Kelly, "The Determination of Child Custody," *The Future of Children* 4 (Spring/Summer 1994) pp. 121–42. Joan Kelly and Michael Lamb, "Using Child Development Research to Make Appropriate Custody and Access Decisions," *Family and Conciliation Courts Review* 38 (2000) pp. 297–311.

73 *in his child's life* Not unexpectedly the joint custody movement met with strong resistance. How could spouses who divorced because they couldn't get along possibly manage to share parenting after divorce? Even in those states where joint custody became an option, judges were still allowed to use their discretion when resolving custody disputes, and many judges refused to grant it because they believed it was not in the best interests of the children. But, championed by angry fathers and liberal divorce reform supporters, the battle for the removal of gender-based custody decisions persisted.

74   *varies from 15 to 22 percent* Child Custody, Divorced Families, 1997. U.S. Census Current Population Survey, National Center for Health Statistics.

74   *as equally shared* One interesting finding I have recently seen cited is that in states that have higher amounts of shared living arrangements, there are also lower levels of divorce. From this finding, it is widely assumed that more parents are staying married rather than have to share their children after divorce. But let's slow down and think about this. The mere fact that two trends are related does not mean that one causes the other. As we've seen, divorce is a highly politicized issue, and myths and stereotypes develop quickly without substantiated data. That parents are less likely to divorce if they know they have to share their children more equally is one of the new myths about divorce.

74   *gender roles of the day* See Constance Ahrons, *The Good Divorce*, for a more in-depth history of custody decisions.

74   *"shadow of the law"* This concept was first introduced by Stanford law professor Robert Minookin in his article coauthored with L. Kornhauser, "Bargaining in the Shadow of the Law: The Case of Divorce, *Yale Law Review*, 88 (1979) pp. 950–97.

75   *arrangements were shared* In total there were twenty-six joint legal custody families (fifty-four children). In total, twenty children from seventeen families spent substantial amounts of time in each household so that they would be considered as having joint *physical* custody. While over half of those parents who shared parenting fairly equally also had legal joint custody, the others were divided among those who legally had father, mother or split custody dispositions. In split custody, each parent is awarded custody of one of more of the children in a family. Although uncommon, it usually occurs when children are old enough to have a voice in who they want to live with or when children are clearly aligned with one parent and have a poor relationship with the other. It is not unusual in these custody awards that girls live with their mothers and boys with their fathers.

76   *years after the divorce*

WHO CHILDREN LIVED
WITH IN THE YEAR FOLLOWING THE DIVORCE

Mother	112
Father	27
Both, alternating	20
Lived Independently	6
Lived at college	4
Got married, lived with spouse	1
With other relatives, friends	1
Missing data	2

76   *after their parents' divorces* The subjects of other long-term studies, such as the ones conducted by Judith Wallerstein and E. Mavis Hetherington, had all lived with their mothers. Although informal shared-parenting arrangements existed, joint custody was not legally available when these studies began.

78   *they were proven unfit* Clearly, in 1979 in the county that I drew this sample from, judges were using their discretion about whether to award joint custody. Although there were four family court judges at the time, I found joint custody families in only two of the judges' jurisdictions. Since judges retain the right to rule on custody decisions, there are at least two possibilities for this: Either two of the judges did not approve joint custody requests or attorneys representing parents who wanted joint custody were careful to schedule their cases on the dockets of those judges known to be supportive.

83   *cope with the crossings* See Myrna Silton-Goldstein, "The Relationship Between Coparenting and Psychological Crossings: An Exploratory Study," doctoral dissertation, The Los Angeles Psychoanalytic Institute (1986).

CHAPTER 5:
FATHERS

97   the *"father problem"* David Blankenhorn, *Fatherless America* (New York: Basic Books, 1995); David Popenoe, *Life Without Father* (New York: Free Press, 1996); and Ross Parke & Armin Brott, *Throwaway Dads* (New York: Houghton Mifflin Co., 1999).

99   *". . . tearing the children apart"* Bob Thompson, "Is This Any Way to Run a Divorce?" *Washington Post Magazine*, November 24, 2002.

105   *soon after the divorce* A discussion of the issues of parental alienation is beyond the scope of this book. To find out more about this topic see Richard A. Warshak, *Divorce Poison* (New York: Regan Books, 2001) and Joan Kelly and Janet Johnston, "The Alienated Child: A Reformulation of Parental Alienation Syndrome," *Family Courts Review*, 39 (2001), pp. 249–66.

CHAPTER 6:
REINVENTING THE BRADY BUNCH

118   *the new extended family* Delia Ephron, *Funny Sauce* (New York: Viking Penguin Inc., 1986).

119   *". . . making your entrance"* Elizabeth L. Post, *Emily Post on Second Marriages* (New York: Harper Perennial, 1991), p. 58.

122–23   *two-stepfamily households together* For an extensive review of the research from 1990 to 2000, see M. Coleman, L. Ganong, and M. Fine, "Reinvestigating remarriage: Another decade of progress," *Journal of Marriage and the Family* 72, no. 4 (2000): 1288–1307.

132   *twenty years down the line*

RATES OF REMARRIAGE TABLE

	By Family* Number of mothers and fathers who remarried		By Children** Numbers of children whose mothers and fathers remarried	
	Number of Mothers who Remarried	Numbers of Fathers who remarried	Mothers	Fathers
One year postdivorce (wave 1)	11 (12%)	21 (24%)	14 (8%)	49 (28%)
Three years postdivorce (wave 2)	34 (38%)	53 (60%)	55 (32%)	109 (63%)
Five years postdivorce (wave 3)	44 (49%)	62 (70%)	72 (42%)	121 (70%)
Twenty years postdivorce (wave 4)	64 (72%)	77 (87%)	109 (63%)	152 (88%)

* $n = 89$ for this column representing the total number of families represented at wave 4 assessment
** $n = 173$ for this column representing the total number of adult child respondents at wave 4

138   *live with their stepchildren full-time* A. Cherlin and F. Furstenberg, "Stepfamilies in the United States," *Review of Sociology* 20 (1994): 359–81.

149   "*. . . it's the stepfamily*" Erma Bombeck, "Here Come the Stepfamilies," *Wisconsin State Journal*, March 25, 1984.

CHAPTER 7:
THE IMPORTANCE OF TRIBAL ELDERS

169   *with each other and their children* Twenty years later all but two of these couples still had amicable relationships.

170   *distress of the earlier times* All but one of these couples continued to be amicable twenty years later.

CHAPTER 8:
FOSTERING RESILIENCE

199 *new information filters in* Although most didn't remember blaming either parent, I was surprised that one-third of the participants did blame one parent, with their fathers being blamed twice as frequently as their mothers. The most frequent reasons they gave for blaming a parent were adultery or alcohol and physical abuse.

201 *at least some of them* Of the 173 children in my study, all but four of the adult children experienced at least one of these transitions and over three-quarters experienced four or more changes in the twenty years since their parents' divorce.

NUMBER OF TRANSITIONS CHILDREN EXPERIENCED

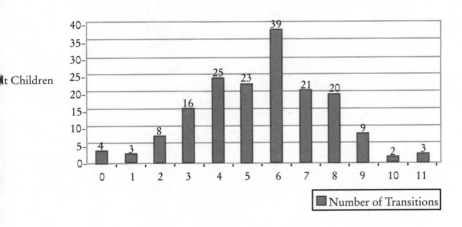

POSTSCRIPT

242 *reduced by 40 percent* E. Jane Costello, Ph.D., Scott N. Compton, Ph.D., Gordon Keeler, MS, Adrian Angold, MRC, "Relationships between Poverty and Psychopathology: A Natural Experiment," *JAMA* 290 (2003): 2023–29.

243 *aimed at fighting change* For more information about the effects of our lack of family policies and the controversies in the national debate, see Ann Hartman, "Families and Social Policy," in Froma Walsh, ed. *Normal Family Processes* (New York: Guilford Press, 2002).

SELECTED REFERENCES

Ahrons, C. R., and J. L. Tanner "Adult children and their fathers: Relationships 20 years after parental divorce." *Family Relations* 52 (2003): 340–51.

Ahrons, C. R. "Divorce and Remarriage: The Children Speak Out." Unpublished research report, Judicial Council of California, 2001.

———."Divorce: An unscheduled life cycle transition." In B. Carter and McGoldrick, eds. *The Family Life Cycle,* 3rd ed. New York: Allyn and Bacon (3rd edition).

———, and Miller, "The effect of the postdivorce relationship on paternal involvement: A longitudinal analysis." *American Orthopsychiatric Association, Inc.* 63 (1993): 441–50.

———. "After the breakup." *Family Therapy Networker* 13 (1989): 31–41. Reprinted in *The Best of the Networker.*

———, and L. Wallisch. "Parenting in the binuclear family: Relationships between biological and stepparents." In K. Pasley and M. Ihinger-Tallman, eds., *Remarriage and Stepfamilies.* New York: Guilford Press, 1987.

———, and L. Wallisch. "The relationship between former spouses." In D. Perlman and S. Duck, eds., *Intimate Relationships: Development, Dynamics, and Deterioration.* Los Angeles: Sage Publications, 1987.

Ahrons, C. R., and A. Sorensen. "Father-child involvement." In J. Trost, C. Szombarthy, and I. Weede, eds., *The Aftermath of Divorce: Coping with Change.* Budapest, Hungary: Akademiai Kaido, 1985.

Ahrons, C. R. "The binuclear family: Parenting roles and relationships." In I. Koch-Nielsen, ed., *Parent-Child Relationship, Post-Divorce*, 54–79. Copenhagen, Denmark: The Danish National Institute for Social Research, 1984.

——— . "Predictors of paternal involvement postdivorce: Mothers' and fathers' perceptions," *Journal of Divorce* 6 (1983): 55–59.

——— . "Divorce: Before, during, and after." In H. McCubbin and C. Figley, eds., *Family Stress, Coping and Social Support*, 102–15. New York: Brunner/Mazel, Inc., 1983.

———, and M. E. Bowman. "Changes in family relationships following divorce of adult child: Grandmothers' perceptions." *Journal of Divorce* 5 (1982): 49–68. Reprinted in D. Olson and B. Miller, eds., *Family Studies Review Yearbook*, vol. 2. Beverly Hills: Sage Publications, 1984.

———, and M. S. Perlmutter. "The relationship between former spouses: A fundamental subsystem in the remarriage family." In L. Messinger, ed., *Therapy with Remarriage Families*, 31–46. Rockville, Md.: Aspen Publishing, 1982.

——— . "The continuing coparental relationship between divorced spouses," *American Journal of Orthopsychiatry* 51 (1981): 315–28. Reprinted in D. Olson and B. Miller, eds., *Family Studies Yearbook*, vol. 2. Beverly Hills: Sage Publications, 1984.

———, and S. Arnn. "Children and their divorced parents: Issues for hospital staff," *Health and Social Work* 6 (1981): 21–28.

——— "Redefining the divorced family: A conceptual framework for postdivorce family system reorganization," *Social Work* 25 (1980): 437–41.

——— . "Divorce: A crisis of family transition and change," *Family Relations* 29 (1980): 533–40. Reprinted in D. Olson and B. Miller, eds., *Family Studies Review Yearbook*, vol. I. Beverly Hills: Sage Publications, 1983.

——— . "Joint custody arrangements in the postdivorce family," *Journal of Divorce* 3 (1980): 189–205.

——— . "The binuclear family: Two households, one family," *Alternative Lifestyles* 2 (1979): 499–515.

——— . "The coparental divorce: Preliminary research findings and policy implications." In A. Milne, ed., *Joint Custody: A Handbook for Judges, Lawyers, and Counselors*. Portland, OR: Association of Family Conciliation Courts, 1979.

Bowman, M. E., and C. R. Ahrons. "Impact of legal custody status on fathers' parenting postdivorce," *Journal of Marriage and the Family* 47 (1985): 481–88.

Crosbie-Burnett, M., and C. R. Ahrons. "From divorce to remarriage: Implications for therapy with families in transition," *Psychotherapy and the Family* 1 (1985): 121–37.

Salka, F. T., and C. R. Ahrons. "New roles for family lawyers in the new world of stepfamilies." *The Family Law News and Review* 7 (1986): 6–12.

ACKNOWLEDGMENTS

F ive years ago, when I first decided to write this book, I was unaware of how many people would join me along the way. It was their support, encouragement, and expertise that made this book possible.

I offer my most heartfelt thanks

To my research staff: Susan Corbin Harris, who supervised the data collection and made the 90 percent response rate a reality. Norella Putney-Hyde, who supervised the data preparation and conducted the preliminary analyses. Jennifer L. Tanner, who joined the project when I was at the Radcliffe Institute, coordinating the longitudinal data set and conducting the data analyses for this book. She also read early drafts and embroidered them with her helpful critiques and suggestions. Hannah Trierweiler, a Harvard student who apprenticed with me as part of the research partnership program, who read every interview and carefully applied qualitative coding methods. All four spent many hours in discussions with me, shaping my thinking by sharing their views, personal reflections and offering their unique insights. Then there were the interviewers, coders and secretarial assistants at USC, who all took that extra step that makes a study of this kind possible.

To Sandra Dijkstra, my literary agent, for her wise counsel and unwavering support. Gail Winston, my editor at Harper-Collins, for her incisive editorial direction, her enthusiasm, and vision. Caroline Pincus, book midwife extraordinaire whose gentle prodding helped me stay on course. Her insights and editorial suggestions helped shape this book and enliven my writing. Christine Walsh and all the HarperCollins folks who spent countless hours bringing this book to publication.

To those who provided financial assistance: Dr. William Sammons, who called out of the blue one day offering a small grant that fortuitously became the impetus to begin this wave of the study. The Foundation for the Contemporary Family and the State of California's Center for Families, Children, and the Courts for their grants that made it possible to move forward and complete the Binuclear Family Study. The Radcliffe Institute at Harvard, which awarded me a fellowship so that I could devote my time to work on this book, and to the Murray Research Center, for providing office space, technical support, and a stimulating research environment. The University of Southern California for granting me a year's leave from my academic and administrative responsibilities and research support throughout the study.

To my friends and colleagues for their continuing support, stimulating discussions, and helpful comments. My family, for being super cheerleaders whose faith sustained me through trying times. To my research and client families, without whom there would be no book. A special thanks to Jennifer and Andrew for enthusiastically agreeing to allow me to include their wedding story.

To Roy, my partner in life, who listened patiently, read and commented on my drafts, kept my computer working, cooked our meals, and kept the house in running order.

And to Geri, Amy, Andy, Mark, Laine, Elly, Jake, and Emma, for being my shining lights.

INDEX